True HAUNTS

Real Paranormal Encounters and True Ghost Stories

Vol 1

Adam C. Norton

Copyright © 2025 by **Adam C. Norton**
All rights reserved.

No portion of this book may be reproduced, stored in a retrieval system, or transmitted in any form by any means—electronic, mechanical, photocopying, recording, or otherwise—without prior written permission from the publisher or author, except for brief quotations in reviews or as permitted by U.S. copyright law.

True Haunts is a copyrighted work and part of an ongoing series. The title *True Haunts* and related branding are pending trademark registration.

This book is a work of non-fiction based on accounts provided by individuals. The author and publisher make no representations or warranties regarding the accuracy, completeness, or reliability of these accounts. The contents of this book are for entertainment purposes only. Neither the author nor the publisher assumes any responsibility for any consequences that may arise from reading this book.

This publication is designed to provide general information on the subject matter covered. It is sold with the understanding that neither the author nor the publisher is engaged in rendering legal, financial, medical, or other professional advice. Readers should consult a qualified professional when appropriate. The author and publisher shall not be liable for any loss or damages, including but not limited to special, incidental, consequential, or other damages.

First Edition 2025
Printed in the United States of America

ISBN: 979-8-9927531-0-3

Published by Lucid Bridge Media
For inquiries, permissions, or to submit a story for future volumes, visit:
www.truehaunts.com

Dedication

To Gabriela -

For your endless patience and unwavering love. Your belief in me and this project has been my greatest source of encouragement. I couldn't be more grateful for the adventure we share.

Introduction

Ghost stories are fun when they're fiction—when you can turn the page, close the book, and leave the fear behind. But what if you couldn't? What if, instead of fading into the dark corners of your mind, the fear followed you home?

True Haunts is a collection of experiences from ordinary people who never expected to encounter the unexplainable. These aren't stories about exploring haunted asylums or chasing spirits through old cemeteries. These are accounts from people who were just living their lives... working late, taking a drive, putting their child to bed... when the impossible happened.

It starts small. A noise you can't explain. A shadow in the corner of your eye. At first, you dismiss it. But then, the moments add up. The fear takes root. Before you know it, you realize... you're not imagining it.

Maybe you've had an experience of your own. Maybe you've felt a chill that had no source. Heard a whisper in an empty room. Maybe you've convinced yourself it was nothing.

These stories will make you question that certainty.

Because the scariest encounters aren't the ones we seek out. They're the ones that find us.

And it can happen to anyone.

Even you.

What is True Haunts?

"The oldest and strongest emotion of mankind is fear, and the oldest and strongest kind of fear is fear of the unknown."
~ H.P. Lovecraft

True Haunts is more than just a collection of ghost stories. It's a record of firsthand encounters with the unknown. Each account comes from someone who has experienced something that defies explanation, something they can't forget.

Unlike urban legends or campfire tales, these stories are personal. They are told in the voices of those who lived them, with all the confusion, fear, and lingering uncertainty that comes with an encounter they never expected. Some seek answers. Others seek validation. But none of them were looking for a ghost story... until they found themselves in one.

These stories follow a pattern: a normal moment, an ordinary setting, disrupted by something unexplainable. Some events unfold gradually, subtle disturbances that build into something undeniable. Others happen in an instant but leave a lasting mark. What ties them together is that they all leave the storyteller forever changed.

If you've ever wondered if something was watching you from the darkness, if you've ever heard a sound that shouldn't have been there, if you've ever felt a presence you couldn't explain—these stories will feel unsettlingly familiar.

And if you have a story of your own, you're not alone. *True Haunts* is a growing archive of encounters, a place where those who have experienced the unexplained can share their truth. If you've had an experience you can't explain, you can submit your story for a future volume. Because every account brings us one step closer to understanding what lurks just beyond our perception.

Share Your Experience

Do you have a story to tell? You're not alone. And neither were they.

Submit Your Story and be included in the next Volume of *True Haunts*!

Scan the QR code:

- *Submit Your Story*

- *Explore the True Haunts series*

Or visit: www.truehaunts.com

About the Author

For Adam Norton, the paranormal started as nothing more than entertainment. A good ghost story was always fun... a thrilling escape into the eerie and unknown. As a child, spooky tales were a source of excitement, but they were just that: fiction. The thought of ghosts and hauntings was intriguing, but never something to be taken seriously.

That belief changed in the early 90s, when Adam moved to Chicago and rented an old house. At first, the strange occurrences seemed like nothing more than misplaced objects... things not being where they were left. But as time went on, those small anomalies escalated. His girlfriend at the time was the first to notice: objects moving on their own, an unsettling presence in the house, and an overwhelming feeling of being watched. At first, Adam dismissed it as imagination... until she moved out, and the activity turned on him. The same experiences, the same eerie phenomena, now impossible to ignore.

By the time he left that house, he was no longer a skeptic.

This was around the time paranormal investigation shows began to gain popularity, and Adam was hooked. He watched them religiously, searching for evidence that mirrored his own experiences, proof that he wasn't alone. Years later, his curiosity led him to join a team of paranormal investigators, where once again, he encountered things he couldn't explain. The validation he found in those moments only deepened his fascination with the unknown.

Now, with *True Haunts*, Adam aims to create something for everyone who shares an interest in the paranormal. Whether you love a chilling ghost story just for the thrill, or you're searching for accounts that resonate with your own unexplained experiences, *True Haunts* is here to collect and share real encounters from real people.... because sometimes, the scariest stories are the ones that actually happened.

Contents

1. The Maintenance Man — 1
2. Always Behind Me — 13
3. The Man My Mother Saw — 19
4. The Vanishing Roommate — 27
5. Morning Commute — 33
6. Something in the Trees — 35
7. The Repeated Knock — 45
8. The Cabin Next Door — 51
9. The Last Shift — 59
10. The Man at the Window — 65
11. The Victorian Renovation — 71
12. The Guest Room — 77
13. The Watcher in the Parking Lot — 83

14.	The Room with the Blue Door	89
15.	The Woman by the Guardrail	97
16.	The Apartment Next Door	103
17.	The Unfinished Call	109
18.	The Wrong Reflection	115
19.	The Car in the Ditch	121
20.	The Stranger in the Background	125
21.	The Unlocked Door	131
22.	The Silent Radio	137
23.	Through Her Eyes	141
24.	The Black-Eyed Visitors	145
25.	The Neighbor's Light	149
26.	The Woman in the Stairwell	153
27.	The Baby Monitor	159
28.	The Customer Who Never Left	165

CHAPTER ONE

The Maintenance Man

"I've worked in this building for years, but what I saw that night still haunts me." ~ Greg, Michigan

I've been working the night shift as a janitor for almost eight months now. It's nothing special, just your standard twelve-story corporate building with endless rows of cubicles, conference rooms, and those break areas with vending machines and microwaves. During business hours, the place is very active, phones ringing constantly, keyboards clicking, people chatting, printers whirring. But after 7 PM? The transition is literally like night and day. It's like someone flipped a switch, and suddenly the building becomes a ghost town.

Most nights it's just me and Carl, the security guard. He's this older guy, maybe mid-sixties, who's been working here since the building opened in the late '90s. Carl does his rounds every couple hours but spends most of his shift in the security office in the lobby, watching monitors or—let's be honest—scrolling his phone or streaming the game. I don't blame him. Nothing ever happens here.

My routine is pretty straightforward. I start at the top floor and work my way down. Empty trash bins, vacuum carpets, wipe down surfaces, clean restrooms, mop tile floors. The same monotonous tasks, night after night. The pay isn't great, but it's steady work. Plus, I've always been a night owl, so the hours suited me fine.

For the first couple months, I actually enjoyed the solitude. There was something peaceful about having this massive building practically to myself. Just me, my cleaning cart, and my wireless earbuds playing podcasts to keep me company. I got into a comfortable rhythm. The whole place became familiar—every squeaky floor tile, every flickering light fixture, every temperamental door hinge.

But then... things started changing. Subtle things at first.

I remember the first incident clearly. It was a Tuesday night in late October. I was on the eighth floor, vacuuming between cubicles, when my earbuds died. Annoyed, I pulled them out and continued working in silence. That's when I noticed it—footsteps. The sound of hard-soled shoes on tile.

I switched off the vacuum, listening. The footsteps continued for a few seconds, then stopped. I thought maybe Carl had come up for an unexpected round.

"Carl? That you, man?"

Nothing. Just that silence that old buildings have at night.

I unplugged the vacuum and walked toward where I'd heard the sound—the hallway leading to the executive offices. Empty. Completely empty.

I shrugged it off. Old buildings make weird noises. Pipes, ventilation systems, the structure settling. That had to be it.

But then it happened again the following week. I was cleaning the glass conference room on the tenth floor when I distinctly heard a chair scrape across the floor in the room next door. It wasn't subtle either; it was the unmistakable sound of metal chair legs dragging across hardwood flooring.

I froze, spray bottle mid-air, heart suddenly pounding. It was nearly midnight. The building had been empty for hours.

"Hello?" "Someone working late?"

Silence again.

I set down my cleaning supplies and cautiously approached the conference room. The door was open, lights off. I reached in, flipped the switch, and the fluorescents came to life.

Empty. Just an oval table surrounded by eight chairs—all perfectly pushed in.

That night, during my break, I mentioned it to Carl. We were both in the lobby, me eating my sandwich, him nursing his thermos of coffee.

"Hey, Carl... you ever hear weird noises in this place at night? Like, footsteps or furniture moving when nobody's around?"

He looked up at me. Then he chuckled, but there was something off about it.

"Oh, that's just the old maintenance man making his rounds."

I laughed nervously, assuming he was joking. "Old maintenance man? What do you mean?"

He looked down at his coffee, swirling it around. "Forget I said anything. Old building, you know? They all make noises."

The way he said it—like he was backpedaling—made my skin prickle. The rest of my break passed in uncomfortable silence, but that comment lodged itself in my brain like a splinter.

For the next few shifts, I tried to ignore the occasional unexplained sounds. The soft rustling of papers in empty offices. The distant sound of a bathroom faucet turning on and off. The elevator humming to life and stopping at floors where no one had called it. I told myself it was just the building's quirks, or maybe my imagination working overtime in the quiet of night.

But then came the night that changed everything.

It was a Friday in mid-November. Rainy, windy—one of those nights where the weather makes everything feel damp and cold. I was up on the tenth floor, working my way through the executive wing. Most nights I saved this area for last because it was always the cleanest—these offices barely looked used compared to the rest of the building.

I'd just finished emptying the trash cans and was about to start vacuuming when I heard it.

"James?"

A voice. Clear as day. Calling a name from somewhere down the dark hallway.

I stood perfectly still, my pulse immediately racing. "Hello? Carl, that you?"

Silence.

I swallowed hard, trying to convince myself I'd imagined it. Maybe it was just the wind outside, or the rain against the windows playing tricks on my ears. But deep down, I knew better. That was a voice—a man's voice—and it had called out a specific name.

"Anyone there?" I tried again, my voice bouncing off the empty walls.

Nothing.

I forced myself to keep working, though my hands had developed a slight tremor. I plugged in the vacuum, determined to finish quickly and move to another floor. As I pushed it across the carpet, I couldn't shake the feeling of being watched. You know that sensation—the prickling at the back of your neck, the hyperawareness of the empty space behind you.

I kept glancing over my shoulder, but the hallway remained empty.

When I finished vacuuming, I gathered my supplies and headed for the supply closet to restock. The tenth-floor closet was at the end of the main corridor—larger than the others, almost like a small room. As I approached, I noticed something odd. The door was slightly ajar, a sliver of darkness between door and frame. I always kept these doors closed and locked—it was part of protocol. But this particular door had a lock that never seemed to work properly

"Get a grip," I muttered to myself, and reached for the door handle.

"James?"

The voice came from inside the closet.

I snatched my hand back like I'd been burned. My heart pounded against my ribs, I could hear it in my ears.

"Who's there?" I demanded, trying to sound confident, when really all I felt was fear.

I was about to bolt for the elevators, but then decided I was being ridiculous. There had to be a logical explanation. Maybe someone was working late and I'd somehow missed them. Maybe they were looking for supplies.

Taking a deep breath, I pushed the door open wider.

The hinges let out this long, slow creak that made my skin crawl.

It was just the supply closet. Shelves stocked with cleaning products, paper towels, trash bags. Extra light bulbs lined up neatly in their boxes. The industrial sink in the corner. Same as always.

In the back, hanging on a wall hook, was an old gray maintenance uniform. I'd noticed before but never gave it much thought. It looked worn.

And there, stitched above the pocket, was a name.

James.

My breath stopped. The same name I'd heard called out. This couldn't be a coincidence.

With my shaking hand, I reached toward the uniform, some part of me needing to touch it, to prove to myself it was real. My fingers were inches from the fabric when—

THUMP.

Something heavy fell behind me.

I spun around so fast I nearly lost my balance. A bucket had toppled from the shelf near the door, now lying on its side on the floor. But there was nothing—no one—that could have knocked it over.

I turned back to the uniform.

It was swaying gently, as if disturbed by a breeze.

But there were no windows in this room. No vents nearby. No source of moving air.

I stood there, frozen, as the reality of the situation crawled over me like ice water. Then I heard it—breathing. Slow, breathing. Right behind me.

It was close. So close I could feel the faintest air on the back of my neck.

My body locked up completely. My brain screamed at me to move, to run, but I was paralyzed. I didn't want to turn around. I really, really didn't want to turn around.

But I had to.

Summoning every ounce of courage, I spun fast to face whatever was there, I wasn't sure my heart could take it.

Nothing. The room was empty. Just me, and that damned fallen bucket.

I took a step backward, bumping into the shelving. I needed to get out. Now.

I reached for the doorknob, desperate to escape.

That's when it hit me—a blast of freezing air so cold it burned my skin. Not just cool air, but a bone-chilling cold that seemed to pass through my clothes, through my skin, into my very core. And with it came a smell—something metallic and stale, like old pennies.

Before I could react, the closet door slammed shut with such force that the shelves rattled. I grabbed the handle, twisting frantically—but it wouldn't budge. The door that never locked was suddenly immovable.

"Help!" I shouted, pounding on the door. "Carl! Anybody!"

Behind me, I heard a soft rustling. The hairs on my arms stood on end.

I don't remember how I got out of that closet. I have flashes—shoulder ramming against the door, suddenly tumbling out into the hallway when the door gave way. I just remember running—full sprint—down the hall, past the elevators (no way I was getting in that enclosed space), and straight for the emergency stairs.

I took those stairs three at a time, nearly falling several times, gasping for breath. By the time I reached the lobby, my legs were weak and shaking so hard I could barely stand.

Carl was at his desk, casually flipping through his phone. He looked up as I burst through the stairwell door.

"Jesus, man, you okay? You look like you've seen a—"

"What's on the tenth floor?" I cut him off, still struggling to catch my breath. "Who's James?"

Carl's face went completely blank for a moment. Then he sighed and put his phone down.

"So you met him, huh?"

Those words sent ice through my veins. I stared at him, unable to process what he'd just said. My mouth opened and closed, but no words came out.

Carl glanced at the security monitors, then back at me.

"Sit down before you fall down," he said, gesturing to the chair beside his desk. "You want some water?"

I shook my head, but I did sit. My legs wouldn't have held me much longer anyway.

"What... who did I meet?" I finally managed.

Carl rubbed his mustache, looking uncomfortable. "James. He was the building's maintenance supervisor when this place first opened. Good guy. Hardworking. Too hardworking, maybe."

I just stared.

"Back in 2001, he was working late. Really late. Past midnight. There was some issue with the HVAC system on—the tenth floor. Boss needed it fixed before a big meeting the next morning." Carl paused. "Nobody else was in the building. Security was different back then—no overnight guard, just cameras. James went up to fix the problem, and... well, he never came back down."

My mouth went dry. "What happened to him?"

"Heart attack," Carl said simply. "They found him the next morning in the supply closet. Doctor said he probably died instantly. He was only 52."

I felt sick. "And you never told me this? Even after I mentioned hearing things?"

Carl shifted uncomfortably. "Look, I've worked here twenty-some years. Every night janitor we've had has experienced something. Some quit after one shift. Others last longer. You seemed... I don't know, more level-headed than most. I figured if you didn't experience anything, why scare you for no reason?"

"But you knew," I said, anger starting to replace fear. "You knew something was in this building, and you just let me work here, night after night, completely unaware."

"He's harmless," Carl said defensively. "In all these years, James has never hurt anyone. He's just... still doing his job, I guess. Making his rounds. Checking on things."

I couldn't believe what I was hearing. Carl was talking about this... this ghost or whatever it was... like it was just another coworker.

"I'm not going back up there," I said firmly. "Not tonight. Not ever."

Carl nodded, understanding.

I didn't sleep at all that weekend. Every time I closed my eyes, I saw that swaying uniform. Heard that voice calling a name—his own name. Felt that icy breath on my neck.

Monday morning, first thing, I requested a transfer to the day shift. I didn't care that it meant a pay cut or that I'd have to work around people. Anything was better than being in that building at night.

My supervisor approved the change, but not without giving me a knowing look. I wasn't the first to make this request, and I wouldn't be the last.

The day shift was better. Surrounded by people, with sunlight coming through windows, the building felt normal. There was no way I was working nights in that building anymore.

I thought moving to the day shift would help. But after a while, it still didn't feel like enough. Eventually, I just had to leave the job completely.

I never even went back, not even to collect my final paycheck. They mailed it to me.

CHAPTER TWO

Always Behind Me

"My grandfather always used to say don't look behind you. I wish I had listened." ~ Anonymous, Florida

I've always been a creature of habit. Same morning routine, same drive to work, same first steps when I get to the office. I get in early, make coffee, check my emails, and settle in before most people even show up. It's nothing exciting, but it's predictable... comfortable.

That's probably why I didn't notice him at first.

He was just another coworker. Friendly, easy to talk to, one of those people who always had some comment about the weather or whatever was going on in the office. We weren't friends or anything, but we crossed paths a lot... breakroom, hallways, waiting for the elevator. Normal stuff.

If you had asked me back then, I would've said I barely thought about him. Just one of those casual work acquaintances, the kind you chat with and then go about your day. But at some point, I started noticing a pattern.

It was always just small talk, but somehow, it kept happening at the exact same moments. I'd be heading out for lunch, and there he was. I'd be the last one in the office, shutting off my computer, and I'd turn to see him walking by. Every single time I walked down that one long, quiet hallway... he was behind me.

Not in a weird way. It was just one of those things where, after a while, you start to pick up on it. How often can you run into the same person before it stops feeling random?

I told myself I was being paranoid. That's what I do sometimes... overthink things. So I shook it off. Just a coincidence.

I was sitting in the breakroom during lunch, talking with a coworker about some random office stuff, when I mentioned him. It was just an off-hand comment...something about how I kept running into him in the hallways.

My coworker gave me this weird look. "Who?"

I said his name, waiting for some kind of recognition. Instead, they frowned and looked confused. "Uh, he hasn't been here in weeks."

I let out a short laugh. "What? No, I just talked to him yesterday. Right over there by the elevator."

They just shook their head. "That's not possible."

Something about the way they said it made my stomach knot. "What do you mean?"

They hesitated for a second, like they weren't sure if they should say it. Then, quietly, "He passed away a couple of weeks ago."

I just stared at them. "What? No... that's not right."

"I'm serious," they said. "It was in the company email and everything. He's gone."

I sat there, not sure what to say. My head felt weird, like I'd suddenly forgotten how to think. That didn't make sense. I had just seen him. I knew I had.

Except... had I? I tried to grab onto a clear memory... something real, something solid... but all I got was flashes. Him walking past me. Him nodding in the hallway. The back of his head as he turned a corner.

I suddenly felt sick. I needed someone else to confirm this was some kind of mistake. For the rest of the day, I asked around, bringing him up in casual conversation. Every single person told me the same thing.

He hadn't been in the office for weeks.

Because he was dead.

I couldn't let it go. The rest of the day, I felt like I was moving in a fog, barely hearing people when they talked to me. As soon as I got back to my desk, I pulled up my emails, scrolling back through weeks of messages. I was expecting to find something... a meeting invite, a forwarded memo, some proof that he had been here.

There was nothing.

No recent emails. No chats. No calendar events.

I checked again, searching his name specifically, convinced I had to be missing something. But the last email I found was over a month old. The last chat, even older.

That didn't make sense. I had just talked to him. I knew I had.

Maybe I was just remembering things wrong. Maybe I was mixing him up with someone else. But the more I thought about it, the worse it got. I kept trying to replay our conversations, to remember specific words, but the memories felt... hollow. I could see him standing there, could picture his mouth moving... but I couldn't hear what he had said.

I needed proof. Something solid.

Since I work in IT, I had access to the security footage, so I pulled it up.

I didn't know what I was expecting to find. Maybe I just wanted to see him, talking to me like I remembered. But the more I clicked through, the more my stomach tightened.

Every clip I checked, the times where I should have seen he and I talking, it was just me. Talking. Gesturing. Laughing at nothing.

I felt something cold settle in my chest.

I clicked to another day. Same thing. I'd be standing in the hallway, nodding like I was listening to someone... but there was no one there.

The worst part was how normal I looked. I was just going through my day, completely unaware that I had been alone the entire time.

It was late. Most of the office had cleared out by now. I needed to get out of there.

I grabbed my bag and headed for the exit, my footsteps echoing in the empty halls. Just as I reached the door, I heard it.

Another set of footsteps. Right behind me.

I turned, but there was no one there.

By the next day, I decided I had to let it go. I was exhausted. Maybe I was just stressed, stretched too thin, making something out of nothing. People misremember things all the time.

So I stuck to my routine. Got through my work. Ignored the urge to check over my shoulder every few minutes. When the office started emptying out for the night, I stayed a little later than usual, finishing up a few last-minute things.

It was just past nine when I finally got up to leave. As I passed by one of the big office windows, something made me glance at my reflection.

I stopped cold.

There, standing just behind me, was him.

I didn't move. I couldn't. My own reflection stared back at me, frozen, like my brain was refusing to catch up to what I was seeing.

Then I turned.

Nothing.

The office was empty.

I walked out fast, my pulse pounding in my ears. I didn't look at the windows again. I just left.

And I didn't come back for a few days.

I never brought it up again. Never mentioned his name, never talked about what I saw. What was I supposed to say? That I had spent weeks talking to someone who wasn't there? That I had seen him in the glass, standing behind me?

No. I wasn't going to be that guy. I pushed it down, buried it, told myself it was over. And for the most part, life went back to normal.

But every now and then, when I'm working late, I still get that feeling. That weight on the back of my neck, like someone is standing too close.

I'm still afraid to look at my reflection in windows or reflective surfaces, because I will worry... if I look too closely... will I see him again?

Chapter Three

The Man My Mother Saw

"You can explain away a lot of things, but not what I saw with my own eyes." ~ Laura, Oregon

You know how people always say kids are more sensitive to supernatural stuff? That they see things adults can't? Well, in my family, it was the opposite. I never saw anything growing up, but my mom... what she saw changed her forever. Changed both of us, really. I'm still trying to make sense of it all, even now.

I guess I should start from the beginning. Back then, my mom worked evenings at the hospital. She'd usually get home around 10 PM, sometimes a bit later if they were short-staffed. We didn't have much money, and it was just the two of us and our mutt, Max, but we had this little ranch house in a quiet neighborhood. Nothing special, but it was home, you know?

I remember the night everything started. I was fifteen, finishing up some reading for English class, when Mom called. Her voice sounded strange, like she was trying too hard to sound normal.

"Hey, sweetie. I'm in the driveway. Could you... turn on the porch light?"

I did, not thinking much of it. When she came in, though, her face was pale. Her hands were trembling as she hung up her keys.

"Mom? What's wrong?"

She tried to smile, but I could tell something was wrong. "Nothing, just... thought I saw someone, that's all."

I pressed her for details. I mean, if someone was creeping around our house, I wanted to know about it. She told me about the man.

"He was just standing there," she said, hugging herself. "Across the street, completely still." She couldn't stop rubbing her arms. "At first I thought maybe he was waiting for someone, or maybe he was lost. But then I noticed his face."

"What about his face?"

"It was weird. It was dark out there, but I could see his face perfectly. And his eyes... He was staring right at me."

I still remember how Max started acting weird that night. He usually slept in the living room, but he kept pacing between windows, whining. When I tried to get him to settle down, he just pressed against my legs, shaking.

That was just the beginning. Over the next few weeks, things started changing. Mom stopped watching TV in the living room after work. She'd go straight to her room instead, but I could hear her moving around in there for hours. The curtains stayed closed all the time now. She started checking the locks over and over, sometimes three or four times a night.

I tried talking to her about it, but she'd wave me off. "Don't worry about it, honey. I'm just being careful." But I could see she wasn't sleeping well anymore.

Then one night, I heard her in the kitchen at like 3 AM. When I went to check on her, she was standing at the window, just staring out through a tiny gap in the curtains.

"He's closer tonight," she whispered, not turning around.

My stomach dropped. "Mom..."

"Every night, he's a little closer." She sounded tired. So tired. "He started across the street. Then he was at the edge of our yard. Now he's..." She stopped.

I looked out, but all I saw was our empty yard in the streetlight. "There's nobody there, Mom."

She just smiled this sad, tired smile. "You can't see him yet. But you will."

I started watching more carefully after that. Not just at night, but during the day too. I noticed things. Like how Max wouldn't go near the front windows anymore—he'd just sit in the hallway, staring at them, growling. It made me nervous. Or how the motion-sensor light in the backyard kept triggering at odd hours, but when I'd look out, there was never anything there.

I even tried talking to our next-door neighbor. She'd lived there forever, knew everything that happened on our street. "Have you noticed anyone hanging around at night?" I asked, trying to sound casual. "Like, just standing around?"

"Sometimes I hear footsteps. Late at night. Like someone walking up and down the street. But when I look? Nothing."

She mentioned she'd installed a security camera after hearing the footsteps, but it never showed anything unusual.

I went to college a few years later, tried to put it all behind me. But every time I called home, I could hear the tension in my Mom's voice, that fear she tried so hard to hide. She never talked about the man directly anymore, but she didn't have to. I knew he was still there.

Finally, after one particularly bad phone call where she could barely keep it together, I decided enough was enough. I drove home that weekend, determined to prove once and for all that she was just being paranoid.

The house looked normal when I pulled up. Same old place, same quiet street. But as soon as I walked in, I knew something wasn't right. The air felt heavy, like right before a storm.

Mom tried to act normal that evening, but I could see how her eyes kept darting to the windows, how she jumped at every little noise. When she went to bed, I settled into the guest room, leaving the curtains open on purpose. I was going to stay up all night if I had to.

I must have dozed off at some point, because suddenly I was jerking awake, my heart pounding. The room was pitch black, but something had woken me. A sound? A movement? I couldn't tell, but my whole body was screaming that I wasn't alone.

Then I heard it... footsteps in the grass outside. Moving right beneath my window.

My whole body went cold. I wanted to look, but I couldn't move. I just sat there, listening to those footsteps.

The footsteps stopped. Right outside my window.

I don't know what made me do it, maybe desperation, maybe anger at whatever was terrorizing my mother, but I forced myself to get up. My legs were shaking so bad I could barely walk, but I made it to the window.

At first, all I saw was darkness. Then my eyes adjusted, and...

He was there, standing in the yard. Just like Mom described. Standing perfectly still, staring directly at me. But his face, it wasn't right. You know when you're trying to remember someone's face, but the details are kind of blurry and wrong? It was like that, except I was looking right at him. Parts of his face kept shifting, like I couldn't quite focus on them. And his eyes... they were just empty spaces where eyes should be.

I stumbled backward, and in the next second, he was gone. Just gone.

I ran to Mom's room, but she was already awake, sitting up in bed.

"You saw him," she said quietly. It wasn't a question.

"We have to do something," I said, my voice shaking. "Call the police, something."

She just shook her head. "It won't help. I've called them before. They don't believe me because nothing shows up on the cameras. Nothing."

This kept going on for several more years. Usually, it was just the man outside, staring. All the time it gets slightly closer. My mom would try not to talk about it, because she didn't want to worry me. But I could always tell he was still there. I think maybe over time she even got used to him.

But a few years later, Mom called me late at night. She was crying, barely able to speak. When I got there, she was huddled in her room, terrified. She told me through tears how he'd been at her window. How his face had pressed against the glass, but it didn't look like a real face. The features were all mixed up, she said, like someone had tried to make a face without knowing what faces were supposed to look like.

We left the next day. Packed what we could carry and went to a hotel. Then I helped Mom find an apartment across town—a third-floor unit with no trees nearby, no streetlights outside the windows. She sold her house, because she had no intention of going back. For a while, things seemed better. She started sleeping again. Started leaving her curtains open during the day.

Then came the night she called me, her voice barely a whisper: "He found me."

I knew without asking. Somehow, he'd followed her. Followed us. Because it wasn't just about the house, it never had been. He was attached to her. To our family.

That's when Mom suggested something I thought was crazy. Instead of ignoring him, instead of running, we had to confront him. Not physically, I don't think he was even physical, not really. But we had to acknowledge him, and then firmly tell him he wasn't welcome.

It felt stupid at first, standing there talking to empty air. But gradually, things started to change. The heavy feeling in the air started to lift. He appeared less and less often, until finally...

He was gone.

We never figured out who, or what, he was, or why he chose us. Sometimes I still catch myself checking windows at night, looking for that strange, shifting face in the darkness. Mom still keeps her curtains closed after sunset, and I can't really blame her.

But he hasn't come back. And if he does... well, at least now we know we're not crazy. At least now we know what we saw was real.

Even if we wish it wasn't.

Chapter Four

The Vanishing Roommate

"I still don't know if it was real." ~ Anonymous, Virginia

People always talk about college dorms being haunted. Old buildings, stressed-out students, urban legends passed down through generations. But what happened in my freshman dorm wasn't like that. This wasn't some vague ghost story about a student who died decades ago. This was something else. Something that wore my roommate's face.

I was eighteen, living in Winters Hall at State. Pretty typical setup, two beds, two desks, barely enough space to turn around. My roommate Jenna and I weren't best friends or anything, but we got along fine. She was a business major, spent most weekends at her boyfriend Matt's apartment off campus. I was pre-med, which meant a lot of late nights studying. It worked out pretty well, actually. We each had our routines, our own space.

The night it started, I was cramming for an organic chemistry exam. Jenna had gone out around eight, saying she'd probably crash at Matt's place.

I studied until my eyes were burning, finally crawling into bed sometime after midnight. The dorm was quiet by then. You know how buildings have their nighttime sounds? I'd gotten used to all that. Actually found it kind of comforting.

I must have fallen asleep pretty quickly. Next thing I knew, I was half-awake, that weird state where you're not sure if you're dreaming. The room was dark except for the blue light from my laptop charger. And there was Jenna, walking toward the door.

Something about the way she moved caught my attention, even in my groggy state. I watched through half-closed eyes as she reached for the door handle, opened it, and stepped through.

I thought it was weird she didn't say anything, but maybe she was trying not to wake me, so I pulled my blanket up tighter, already drifting back to sleep.

Then my phone buzzed.

I almost ignored it, but it might have been my mom. She'd been having health issues, so I always checked. I grabbed my phone, squinting at the bright screen.

It was a text from Jenna: "Stayed at Matt's, be back tomorrow."

I stared at the message, my brain trying to process what I was seeing. The timestamp said 12:47 AM. I'd just watched Jenna leave our room. But if she was at Matt's...

I sat up, suddenly wide awake. The room was empty, Jenna's bed still neatly made from morning. The door was closed. And it was freezing... I could see my breath in the air.

I told myself I must have dreamed it. Stress, exhaustion, too much caffeine—pick your explanation. But I couldn't shake the image of her walking out. It had felt so real.

The next morning, I tried to play it cool. When Jenna came back, I casually asked if she'd stopped by the dorm at all during the night.

She frowned, dropping her bag on her bed. "No, I told you I was staying at Matt's. Why?"

"No reason," I said quickly. "Just thought I heard something."

But things started changing after that night. I'd wake up at random times, that same bone-deep cold settling over the room. Sometimes I'd hear things—soft footsteps, the sound of someone sitting on Jenna's bed, the rustle of papers on her desk. Once I woke up to find her closet door standing open, clothes pushed to one side like someone had been looking through them.

I started leaving my desk lamp on at night. Started checking the door was locked before bed, then checking it again when those midnight noises woke me up. Jenna noticed—how could she not?—but I brushed it off, saying the light helped me feel safer in general.

Then came the night that changed everything.

It was a Friday. Jenna was at Matt's, as usual. I'd been having trouble sleeping, jumping at every little noise, so I decided to just stay up. I lay in bed with my phone, pretending to sleep but really watching, waiting.

Around 1 AM, the temperature plummeted. And then the door opened.

No one turned the handle. No one unlocked it. It just... opened, smooth and silent.

I watched, paralyzed, as Jenna walked in.

Except... it wasn't really Jenna. I mean, it looked like her—same height, same hair, same clothes she'd been wearing earlier. But the movements were wrong. It walked straight to her bed, sat down facing the wall, and went completely still.

My hands were shaking so bad I could barely type, but I managed to text Jenna: "Where are you right now?"

Her response came immediately: "At Matt's place. Everything ok?"

The thing on Jenna's bed didn't move. Didn't breathe. Just sat there, a perfect silhouette in the darkness.

I don't know what made me do it... fear, maybe, or just the desperate need to prove to myself I was imagining things. I turned on my phone's flashlight and pointed it at Jenna's bed.

The bed was empty.

But in that split second before the light hit, I swear I saw it turn its head. Not toward me... all the way around, like an owl. And its face... it had Jenna's features, but they were all wrong, like someone had tried to arrange them from memory and gotten the spacing wrong.

I didn't sleep that night. Or the next. When I finally told Jenna what was happening, she laughed it off. Said I was stressed, that maybe I should talk to someone about anxiety. But I saw the way she looked around the room, like she was trying to catch something moving in the corners of her vision.

A week later, she announced she was moving off campus. Said she needed more space, more privacy. But the night before she moved out, I woke up to find her sitting straight up in bed, staring at her desk. When I asked what was wrong, she whispered, "I saw someone sitting there. Someone who looked like me."

They assigned me a new roommate, this girl named Beth. Nice enough, but I couldn't relax. Every night, I'd wake up expecting to see that wrong version of Jenna walking through our door. The cold would settle in, and I'd lie there, wondering if tonight would be the night it came back.

I moved out at the end of the semester. Couldn't take it anymore. But here's the thing—a few months later, I ran into Jenna at a coffee shop. We got to talking, and after a few minutes, she looked at me with this strange expression.

"You know what's weird?" she said. "Ever since that semester, people keep telling me they've seen me places I've never been. My sister swears she saw me walking through her house at 3 AM last month, but I was in Florida on spring break."

I didn't know what to say. What could I say? That maybe whatever had been pretending to be her in our dorm room had decided to expand its territory? That it was still out there, still wearing her face?

I've been out of college for three years now. I live alone... can't handle having roommates anymore. Sometimes I still wake up in the middle of the night, that familiar cold settling over my room. And sometimes, in that moment between sleep and waking, I think I hear footsteps. Slow, mechanical footsteps, like something that's still learning how to walk like a human.

I never turn on the light anymore when that happens. I'm too afraid of what I might see—or worse, what might see me. Because now I know: sometimes the things that look like people aren't people at all. And sometimes they learn to copy us a little better each time they try.

Chapter Five

Morning Commute

"I don't check my rearview mirror anymore. Not after what I saw on that highway." ~ Kevin, Wisconsin

I commute to work early, like, really early. I'm usually on the road by 5:30 AM because I hate traffic. This happened last winter, so it was still completely dark out. I was on this stretch of highway I've driven literally hundreds of times, just kind of zoned out like you get on a familiar route, when I saw someone walking on the shoulder.

At first, I didn't think much of it. I mean, it's weird to see someone walking on the highway that early, but whatever. But as I got closer, I realized they were walking really weird. Like, too smooth? I don't know how else to describe it. Their feet were moving, but it was like they were gliding.

I moved over to the left lane - I always give pedestrians plenty of space. As I passed them, I glanced over. They turned their head to look at me, and... okay, this is the part where people always think I'm making it up. Their face was totally normal, just this middle-aged guy, but he was completely gray. Not pale, not like he was sick. Gray.

I looked back at the road for maybe two seconds, then checked my rearview mirror. He was gone. Just gone. There's nowhere he could have gone - it was just open highway with those big sound barrier walls on both sides.

I probably would have convinced myself I imagined it, except about a week later, my coworker was asking if anyone else takes Highway 16 to work. Turns out she'd seen the exact same thing. Same spot, same weird walking, same gray person. We compared times - she leaves about 20 minutes later than me usually.

The really freaky part? When she saw my face as she was telling the story, she stopped and said "You've seen him too, haven't you?"

Once - and this is the last time I ever looked in my rearview mirror after passing him - he was standing in the middle of my lane, just watching my car drive away.

CHAPTER SIX

Something in the Trees

"I used to love the woods. I used to." ~ John, Montana

We had been talking about this trip for weeks. Just me and Jake, two nights in the woods, no cell service, no distractions. A break from work, from people, from everything. We picked the most remote spot we could find, way off the main trails, somewhere we could actually feel like we were in the wild.

The drive out was long, winding through endless trees, the road getting narrower until it was barely more than a dirt path. By the time we parked and started hiking to our campsite, the sun was dipping lower. It was quiet out there. This was real silence, just wind in the trees and the occasional rustling of something in the underbrush.

We set up camp without any trouble. Pitched the tent, gathered firewood, got a good blaze going before it got too dark. The air was crisp, clean in a way that made you want to breathe deeper. For a while, everything was perfect. We cooked dinner over the fire, cracked a couple of beers, and just sat there, talking about nothing.

But after a while, I noticed something. Every so often, Jake would glance past me, his expression shifting just slightly, like he thought he saw something. It wasn't much, just a look of unease before he laughed at whatever joke I was telling and shook it off.

Then I caught myself doing the same thing.

The woods stretched out beyond the firelight, endless black between the trees. Every now and then, I thought I saw movement. Not big, obvious shapes, just tiny shifts, like something was just out of sight, staying just at the edges where the firelight didn't quite reach.

Neither of us said anything about it. There could've been any number of animals out there… deer, raccoons, even a stray coyote. When you're used to background noise all the time, real quiet can mess with your head.

Eventually, the fire burned low, and the night got colder. We put out the last of the embers and climbed into the tent.

I remember lying there, listening to the wind, the occasional creak of branches. Everything was still. Peaceful.

But just before I drifted off, I had the weirdest thought.

Even with my eyes closed, I couldn't shake the feeling that something was out there. Not moving, not making a sound... just there.

The first night should've been uneventful. But a few hours after we crawled into the tent, I woke up to something crunching in the leaves outside.

I lay there, listening. It wasn't the wind. Something was circling the tent. I held my breath, waiting to hear if Jake had noticed, but he was out cold.

My first thought was that it was an animal. A deer, maybe, or something smaller nosing around for food. But the longer I listened, the more I doubted that. It was just outside the tent walls.

I whispered Jake's name, nudging his arm. He groaned, half-awake, until I hushed him. "Listen."

For a second, there was nothing. Just the wind through the trees. Then... another step. Closer this time.

Jake sat up fast, rubbing his face. "What the hell was that?"

I reached for the flashlight. "I don't know. Probably an animal."

He grabbed the zipper of the tent and, very slowly, pulled it open just enough for me to stick my head out and sweep the flashlight around.

Nothing.

Just trees and darkness. No movement, no sound. The second the beam swept across the area, whatever was out there was gone.

We sat there for a few minutes, listening, but the woods were dead silent again. Eventually, Jake let out a breath and shook his head. "We're being dumb. It was probably a raccoon."

I nodded, even though in my gut that didn't feel right. We zipped the tent back up and tried to sleep, but I don't think either of us really did.

The next morning, we didn't talk about it much. We ate breakfast, then decided to explore the area a little.

We found some wood carvings.

They were on a handful of trees near our campsite... deep scratches in the bark, almost like tally marks. At first, we figured they were just from other campers, people marking the trees for whatever reason. There are no bears in this area.

Jake ran a hand over one of them and smirked. "Creepy as hell. Probably some hiker messing with people."

I tried to laugh along, but something about them didn't sit right. I don't know why, but standing there, looking at those marks, I felt... noticed.

Like someone knew we were there.

The second night, we were more on edge. We didn't really talk about it, but we both knew we had slept terribly. Every little noise outside had put us on alert, and neither of us wanted to admit how uneasy we felt.

Still, we stuck to the plan. Ate dinner, sat around the fire, and tried to enjoy it. But the woods felt different now. Quieter.

Then we heard it again.

Footsteps, moving through the brush. Heavier this time.

Jake froze mid-sentence. We both listened. It didn't sound like an animal rummaging around. Back and forth. Slow. Steady.

Jake grabbed the flashlight. "Screw this," he muttered and shined it toward the sound.

Nothing.

No movement, no sign of anything out of place. But the second he turned the light off, we heard it again. Closer now.

"It's gotta be a deer," I whispered, but even I didn't believe it.

The feeling of being watched was unbearable. Every nerve in my body was screaming at me to get up, to move, to run. But where? We a couple of miles from the car, surrounded by nothing but trees.

Neither of us wanted to sit out there anymore. We put the fire out and went straight to the tent, zipping it up fast.

Lying there in the dark, every rustling leaf, every snapped twig sent a jolt of fear through me. Jake wasn't asleep either... I could hear his breathing, slow and tense, like he was listening just as hard as I was.

Neither of us said anything. But I know we were both thinking the same thing.

We were not alone out there.

The next morning, I woke up feeling like I hadn't slept at all. Judging by the way Jake groaned when he sat up, he hadn't either. The tent felt stuffy, and the second I unzipped it, a rush of the morning cold air made me shiver. But then I noticed something else.

I stepped outside. Our campsite... wasn't how we left it.

Nothing was missing, but things weren't where we had put them. Our backpacks had been moved, not far, just shifted enough that it was obvious.

The extra firewood we stacked was scattered. One of the camp chairs had been knocked over. And the fire pit...

It looked like someone had kicked through the ashes.

Jake stood beside me, rubbing his face. "Did you do this?"

"No... did you?"

He shook his head. We both knew the answer.

"Had to be an animal," he muttered, but he didn't sound convinced.

I glanced around, looking for tracks, hoping to see the kind of prints that would make sense. Deer, maybe. A coyote.

But what I saw made my heart sink.

A set of footprints, pressed into the dirt near the fire pit. Bare. Human.

I stared at them. Maybe a hiker? Maybe someone passed through in the night? But who wanders barefoot through the woods in the freezing cold?

Jake saw them too. I could tell by the way his whole body went still. "Man... this is weird."

I nodded slowly. "Yeah."

We stood there, neither of us sure what to do.

"Let's eat," Jake finally said, forcing a laugh. "We're overthinking this."

I didn't argue. I wanted to believe that too.

But I knew something wasn't right.

That night, the fire burned low, barely more than glowing embers, but neither of us wanted to put it out. We sat there, not really talking, just listening.

Every so often, a twig would snap in the distance. A rustle in the brush. We told ourselves it was the wind, the wildlife... the normal sounds of the forest settling for the night. But it never felt that way.

We were being watched. I knew it. Jake knew it. But saying it out loud would make it real.

At some point, exhaustion won out, and we crawled into the tent. We just zipped up the tent and lay there, wide awake, staring at the nylon above us.

I don't know how much time passed before I heard it.

Breathing... just outside the tent.

I stiffened, barely daring to inhale. Jake had heard it too. I could feel him go rigid beside me. The sound was close, way too close. Each breath was long and labored, like whoever... whatever... was out there had been walking for a long time.

Neither of us moved. We just listened.

The breathing shifted, moving from one side of the tent to the other. My skin crawled. The thin nylon between us and it felt like nothing at all.

Jake swallowed hard. "We... we should look," he whispered, barely audible.

I didn't want to. Every instinct told me to stay still, to wait it out. But the breathing was getting closer, right near my head now. I reached for the flashlight, fingers shaking, and nodded.

Jake moved first, inching his hand toward the zipper. The second it started to slide down, the breathing stopped.

Everything went silent.

Jake hesitated, then yanked the tent open. I clicked the flashlight on, shining it out into the darkness.

For a second, there was nothing. Just trees, stretching into the night. But then...

At the very edge of the light, just beyond the fire pit, something stood at the tree line.

Tall. Gaunt. Completely still.

I couldn't see its face. Couldn't make out any features at all.

The light barely touched it before it moved. Fast. Too fast. One second it was there, and the next, it was gone, slipping into the trees.

Jake let out a shaky breath. "Nope. No. We're leaving at first light."

I couldn't even respond. I just kept staring at the trees, gripping the flashlight like it was the only thing keeping us safe.

The fire had almost gone out now. And I knew... whatever was out there... it was watching and waiting.

We didn't sleep. We just sat there in the tent, barely breathing, gripping the flashlight like it was the only thing keeping us safe. Every tiny noise outside made my heart pound. A rustling leaf, a shift in the wind... each one felt like it could be the moment whatever was out there decided to come closer.

Neither of us spoke. We didn't need to. We were both thinking the same thing... waiting for the sky to lighten, for any sign that the night was finally over.

The moment we saw the first hint of dawn, we moved. We tore through camp, stuffing our gear into our packs without even bothering to fold the tent properly. Anything that took too long to pack, we left behind. Food, even Jake's favorite camp chair... it didn't matter. We just needed to go.

The hike back to the car was the longest walk of my life. Every step, I expected to hear something following us. I kept glancing over my shoulder, scanning the trees, waiting to see movement. But there was nothing. Just the endless, empty forest.

When we finally reached the car, we didn't even talk about it. We just got in and drove.

The first hour of the drive was dead silent. Then Jake let out a shaky laugh, more forced than anything. "That was messed up, man."

I nodded, staring straight ahead. "Yeah."

Neither of us could put it into words. We went over it, again and again, trying to make sense of it. Maybe it was some kind of animal. Maybe it was another camper messing with us. Maybe we were just exhausted, hearing things that weren't really there.

Then we started looking things up. Local legends, missing persons reports... anything that might explain what we saw.

Nothing did.

All I know is there was something in those woods, and whatever it was... it was watching us way before we ever saw it.

We haven't been camping since.

Chapter Seven
The Repeated Knock

"The knock came again." ~ Eric, Illionis

The first time it happened, I barely paid attention.

I was in the middle of a movie, half-asleep on the couch, when I heard three knocks on the front door. Not loud, not urgent... just knocking. I figured it was a package delivery, even though it was late. By the time I got up and checked, the porch was empty. No box, nothing.

Probably kids messing around. It was a quiet street, but still, every neighborhood has those kids.

But then it happened again the next night. Same time. Three knocks.

I got up quicker this time, thinking I could catch whoever it was. But when I yanked open the door, there was no one there. The street was still, dark, no movement anywhere.

This went on for a few nights. Always three knocks. Always around the same time. I stopped checking right away, figuring whoever was doing it would get bored and move on. But it didn't stop.

By the fifth or sixth night, I was getting pissed off. I kept my porch light on, hoping that would deter them. It didn't. I even sat by the door, waiting, thinking I'd rip it open fast enough to catch them in the act. But the second I swung the door open... nothing. Just that empty street, as quiet as ever.

I brought it up to my neighbor one evening, just in passing. "You ever have kids messing with your door at night?"

He gave me this weird look. "Why?"

"It's been happening all week. Three knocks, around the same time, every night."

He went quiet for a second, like he was debating something. Then he said, "That's weird. The guy who lived there before you... he used to complain about the same thing."

I laughed. "Seriously?"

He just shrugged. "Don't know much about it. He moved out kinda suddenly. Didn't really tell anyone why."

That stuck with me more than I wanted to admit. But I wasn't about to let some dumb coincidence get to me.

A few nights later, a storm rolled in. Heavy rain, strong winds. One of those nights where no one in their right mind would be outside. I remember sitting in bed, listening to the wind howl, feeling relieved. There was no way it was happening tonight.

Then, right on time... three knocks.

Steady.

Like the storm didn't matter at all.

That night, I decided I was done playing games.

I set up in a chair near the front door, lights off, phone in hand, waiting. I wasn't going to sit there all night... just long enough to prove to myself that this was all some dumb prank.

When the time came, I sat up straighter, watching the door. And right on schedule... three slow knocks.

I jumped up, yanked the door open.

Nothing. No movement, no sound, just the empty street stretching out in front of me.

I stepped outside, scanning the area. No sign that anyone had been near my house at all.

That was the first time I felt something close to fear.

The next day, I bought a security camera.

I mounted it above the door, made sure it was angled just right, and let it record overnight. When I checked the footage the next morning, I felt a weird mix of relief and frustration... nothing. No movement. No knocking. Just an empty porch.

Maybe it was a fluke. Maybe the camera just happened to miss something.

So, I bought another one. This time, I put it inside, facing the door from the hallway.

That night, when the knocking started, I was ready. I grabbed my phone and pulled up the live feed.

The outside camera showed nothing.

But on the inside camera, I saw the door. And with every knock, it visibly shook.

Like someone was hitting it hard. Like someone was standing there.

But there was no one on the other side.

I watched the footage over and over, trying to make sense of it, but the more I watched, the worse it got.

Because whatever was knocking... wasn't there.

The knocking got worse.

It wasn't just three knocks anymore. It would start the same way... but then it would come again, harder, rattling the door in its frame. Some nights it would happen twice. Some nights it would last longer. It didn't make sense. It didn't follow any pattern I could figure out. It just kept happening.

And then, one night, it changed.

I was in bed, half-asleep, when I heard it. Three knocks. But not at the front door.

Inside the house.

I shot upright, my whole body frozen. The sound had come from the hallway.

Three slow knocks.

On my bedroom door.

I didn't know what to do. I just sat there, staring at the door, waiting for something… anything… to happen. And then, the handle twitched.

I didn't wait. I grabbed my keys off the nightstand and pressed my back against the wall, eyes locked on the door. The handle twitched again, just slightly, like someone testing it. My chest felt tight, every part of me screaming to run, but I couldn't go through that door… not with whatever was on the other side.

So, I did the only thing I could think of… I climbed out the window.

The second my feet hit the ground, I took off, running barefoot across the yard, not stopping until I was in my car, hands shaking as I fumbled with the keys. I started my car and sped off, not sure at first even where to go.

I stayed with a friend for a few days after that. I didn't tell him everything. Just that something had freaked me out, that I needed a break from the house. I wasn't sure I'd ever go back.

But eventually, I did.

Everything in the house was exactly the way I left it. No open doors, no broken locks, nothing was missing. But it felt different, and I didn't like it.

Even now, I can't explain it. I never heard the knocking again because I never gave it the chance. I broke my lease, packed up, and left that house behind.

Chapter Eight
The Cabin Next Door

"We thought we were alone out there." ~ *Emi, Vermont*

The drive up to the cabin was half the fun. Just the five of us, packed into Noah's car, music blasting, winding through endless roads surrounded by nothing but trees. No towns, no gas stations... just miles of empty forest. Exactly what we wanted.

We had been planning this trip for weeks... just a weekend away from everything, no service, no responsibilities, just hiking, drinking, and doing a whole lot of nothing. When we finally pulled up to the cabin, it looked perfect. A little worn down, sitting right on the edge of the woods, but cozy enough.

We unpacked fast, calling dibs on rooms, shoving snacks into cabinets, cracking open the first round of beers before we even finished settling in. It felt good. Like we had the whole world to ourselves.

That's when Olivia pointed it out.

"I thought this place was supposed to be the only cabin out here," she said, nodding toward the trees.

A little ways off, past the clearing, there was another cabin. Dark, run-down, and half-hidden behind the trees. The rental listing had mentioned an old abandoned cabin nearby, but looking at it now, it didn't seem as empty as it should have.

There was a light. Just the faintest glow coming from one of the windows.

"Maybe someone is doing some work on it, trying to get it suitable to rent out again," Noah said, but he didn't sound convinced.

The rest of the night was easy. We built a fire, drank too much, played a dumb card game that had us laughing until we couldn't breathe. It was the kind of night we had come here for.

The next morning, we were all moving slow, recovering from the night before. Over coffee, Olivia brought up the cabin next door again.

"That light we saw last night... it was weird, right?"

"Yeah, a little," Noah admitted. "But it was probably someone was working, and then forgot to turn out the light when they left."

"Or," Matt grinned, "we were being watched."

He said it like a joke, but nobody laughed.

We all looked toward the other cabin. In daylight, it looked even worse—boards warped, windows clouded with dust, the whole thing just sitting there like it had been forgotten. It didn't seem like anyone had been near it in years.

"Let's check it out," Olivia said.

It wasn't like we had anything better to do, so we walked over. The front door was locked. We peeked through the windows, but it was hard to see much past the grime. Inside, it was just old furniture, covered in dust. No signs of life. And now, there was no light.

"See?" Noah said. "Nothing creepy. Just an old cabin."

"Or," Matt grinned again, "we were being watched."

That night, after dinner, we were sitting around the fire when Olivia suddenly tensed. "Did anyone else see that?"

We all turned to look. She was staring at the other cabin, eyes locked on one of the windows.

"I swear I just saw something move."

We all stared, waiting. The window was dark, nothing but stillness inside.

"It was probably just a reflection... or maybe an animal got inside," Noah said.

The debate started almost as soon as the fire was lit.

"Okay, so let's just say... what if there actually was someone in that cabin?" Olivia asked, hugging her knees to her chest.

Noah said. "There's no signs of anyone there. We checked."

"Maybe we just didn't check well enough," Matt muttered, staring into the flames.

Nobody had an answer to that. The idea stuck with us, hanging over the conversation like a cloud. We tried to push past it, joking around, playing music, but the mood was different.

I don't know what woke me up. But I opened my eyes and just knew I wasn't alone.

I turned my head toward the window, and saw it.

A figure. Standing outside. Right near the other cabin.

It wasn't moving. Just standing there, perfectly still, barely more than a shadow against the trees. I couldn't see a face, couldn't make out any details, but I could feel it watching.

My whole body went cold. I wanted to look away, to blink and make it disappear, but I couldn't.

Then, finally, I forced myself to move. Shaking Noah's shoulder. "Wake up. Wake up, there's someone out there."

He groaned, pushing my hand away, but when he saw my face, he sat up fast. "What?"

I pointed to the window. "By the other cabin. I swear to God, someone's standing there."

He leaned over to look. And just like that... it was gone.

Nothing.

The next morning, we went straight to the other cabin.

We didn't talk about it much. Nobody wanted to admit how freaked out we were, but we all had the same idea. We needed to check. Maybe there was some explanation, maybe we missed something the first time.

But nothing had changed.

The door was still locked. The dust on the windows was undisturbed. No footprints, no signs that anyone had been inside. It looked exactly the same as it had before. But that didn't make me feel any better.

That night, we were quieter than usual. None of us wanted to be the first to bring up what we were all thinking. We tried to act normal... played cards, made drinks... but every few minutes, someone would glance toward the other cabin. Just in case.

Then, just as we were winding down for the night, we heard it.

A knock.

Right at our front door.

Nobody moved.

Another knock.

We all looked at each other. No one wanted to be the one to open the door.

Noah finally stood up, moving slowly. He pulled the door open just enough to peek outside.

Nothing.

The porch was empty. The trees swayed gently in the wind, but there was no one there.

Then Matt said, "Look."

We turned to follow his gaze. Across the clearing, the other cabin's front door was wide open.

"We have to check it," Matt said, already moving toward the door.

"Are you out of your mind?" Olivia snapped. "Someone is messing with us. You really want to go out there?"

Noah locked the door. "No one is going outside."

We argued for a while. Nobody wanted to admit how scared they were, but it was obvious. Every sound outside had us glancing at each other, waiting for someone to say what we were all thinking.

We were trapped.

Eventually, the conversation died down. We just sat there, staring at the walls, listening.

Hours passed. The exhaustion of the night started catching up with us. We were still scared, but nothing else had happened. Enough time had passed that I just started to relax a little.

And then...

A knock.

Loud. Right against the back window.

Nobody moved.

I didn't want to look. I didn't want to know what was standing behind us, just on the other side of the glass. I could feel it... someone or something was there.

Olivia squeezed her eyes shut. "Don't check. Don't check."

We didn't. We just sat there, frozen, waiting for whatever came next.

But nothing did.

We stayed like that until the sky outside started to lighten, every second stretching unbearably long.

The moment dawn broke, we were out of there.

The second the first streaks of sunlight hit the trees, we were moving. No one said much… we just grabbed our stuff, shoving things into bags. We just needed to go.

The drive back was dead silent at first. Everyone was wired, still caught between exhaustion and adrenaline. It wasn't until we hit the main road that Olivia finally spoke.

"We should tell the rental company."

Noah let out a short breath. "And say what? That we got spooked by an old cabin?"

"Someone knocked on our door," she shot back. "Someone opened that other cabin. We're not making that up."

No one argued after that.

Later that day, once we were home, Noah sent an email to the rental company. He kept it simple… just said we had weird experiences, thought maybe someone had been messing with us, and wanted to let them know.

The response came a few hours later.

The other cabin, according to them, had been abandoned for over a decade. No electricity. No running water. And the doors?

Nailed shut, because they wouldn't stay closed.

We read the email three times, sitting there in stunned silence.

I don't know what we heard out there. I don't know what we saw.

But I know we weren't alone.

Chapter Nine
The Last Shift

"No one believes me, but I know what I saw." ~ Anonymous, Ohio

I still have trouble talking about what happened during my last night shift. Most people probably wouldn't believe me anyway, but honestly, that's not why I hesitate to tell this story. It's more that... when I think about it too much, I start noticing things in the corners of my vision again. Start checking over my shoulder more than I should. So I try not to think about it.

But yeah, okay. Let me tell you what happened.

I'd been working nights at this little 24 hour convenience store for about eight months. Nothing fancy, just one of those places that stays open late even though hardly anyone ever comes in after nine. My shift started at ten, and I'd be there alone until morning. Just me, restocking shelves, doing inventory, making sure everything looked decent for the day crew.

At first, I actually kind of liked it. I mean, who wouldn't want to get paid to basically just hang out by yourself all night? I'd put on my headphones, take my time with the tasks, and honestly just zone out most of the time. The store wasn't big - just six aisles, a small stockroom in the back, and this tiny break room that smelled like old coffee no matter how many times I wiped down the counters.

I guess the first weird thing I noticed was the front doors. They were automatic, you know? And they'd sometimes slide open when nobody was there. Like, I'd be in the middle of restocking cereal or whatever, and I'd hear that soft whoosh sound. I'd look up, and they'd just be standing open, like they were waiting for someone to walk in. After a few seconds, they'd slide shut again.

I didn't think much of it at first. Automatic doors do that sometimes, right? Sensors get dusty or whatever. But after a while, I started noticing it was happening more often.

Then there were the lights in the stockroom. They were on one of those motion sensors to save energy, but they started acting weird. Like, I'd be up front at the register, and I'd see them flip on out of nowhere. When I'd check the security cameras, there'd be nothing back there. Just an empty room with the lights suddenly on.

I remember this one night, I was doing my usual 2 AM snack break, sitting at the register and scrolling through my phone, when I heard this... shuffling sound. Like someone walking really slowly through one of the aisles. I figured maybe a mouse had gotten in - it happened sometimes in older buildings like this. But when I went to check, there was nothing there. Just this weird feeling, like I'd just missed something.

That's when other stuff started happening. Small things at first, but... looking back, I should've paid more attention. I'd spend an hour making sure all the shelves were faced perfectly - you know, all the products pulled to the front, labels facing out - and I'd go do something else for a while. When I came back, things would be pushed back or turned around. Not knocked over or anything dramatic. Just... moved. Just enough that I knew I hadn't left them that way.

The stockroom doors were another thing. I always made sure they were shut tight because they'd make this annoying creaking sound if they were left open. But every so often, I'd glance back and see them standing open just a crack. I started making a point to really pull them closed, even giving them a little tug afterward to make sure. Didn't matter. They'd still end up open.

I tried to rationalize it, you know? Old building, weird drafts, whatever. But it was getting harder to ignore the way my skin would prickle sometimes, like someone was standing right behind me. The way the air would suddenly go cold in certain spots, even though the AC barely worked in that place.

Then came that last night.

I was doing the usual restocking, trying to get through it quickly because honestly, the store had started feeling different after midnight. Like it was too quiet, too empty. I had my headphones in, music turned up maybe a little louder than necessary, when I felt it.

You know that sensation when someone's watching you? That heavy feeling on the back of your neck? Yeah. That hit me so hard I actually stumbled, nearly dropping the box of inventory I was holding. I yanked my headphones out and just... listened.

The store was dead silent. No hum from the coolers, no buzz from the fluorescent lights. Nothing.

Then I heard it. This soft, deliberate tapping sound, coming from the end of the aisle. Like someone slowly dragging their knuckles across the metal shelving.

"Hello?" My voice came out steadier than I expected. "Someone there?"

Nothing. The tapping stopped.

I forced myself to walk toward the sound, telling myself I was being stupid. The store was empty. I knew it was empty. I'd been here alone for hours.

I turned the corner, and the fluorescent light above me flickered. Just once. Just enough to make the shadows shift.

Nothing there. Just shelves of products, everything exactly where it should be.

I let out this shaky laugh, already feeling dumb for getting spooked. But then...

Another tap. This time from the aisle I'd just left.

I spun around so fast I knocked something off the shelf. The sound of it hitting the floor seemed way too loud in the silence.

Still nothing there. But now the air felt... heavy. Like the whole store was holding its breath.

My heart was pounding so hard I could hear it. I took a step back, then another, my eyes darting between the aisles. I needed to get to the front, to the register where I could see all the security cameras.

Then the lights started going out.

Not all at once. One by one, starting from the back of the store, each row of fluorescents clicking off. Like something was moving toward me, bringing the darkness with it.

I ran. I'm not going to pretend I was brave about it. I straight up sprinted to the front of the store, practically diving behind the register. My hands were shaking so bad I could barely pull up the security feed.

The cameras showed nothing. Just empty aisles, half of them now dark.

But then... I saw something on the stockroom camera. A shadow, just at the edge of the frame. It moved like... God, I don't even know how to describe it. Not like a person. More like smoke, but with purpose. It drifted forward, then suddenly...

The screen went black.

All of them did. Every monitor, just... dead.

Nothing but silence. Even the usual hum of the coolers was gone.

And then I heard it. Footsteps. Slow, heavy footsteps coming from the darkness at the back of the store.

They were getting closer.

I didn't know what to do. I just sat there, watching the darkness, listening to those steps. They were so heavy, so steady. Like whatever was coming didn't need to hurry.

The last row of lights went out.

In that final moment of fluorescent light, I saw something. A figure, standing at the end of aisle three. Tall. Too tall. And dark, like it was made of shadows.

It turned its head toward me.

I don't remember running to my car. Don't remember driving home. I just know I ended up there, somehow, shaking so badly I couldn't control it.

I called my manager the next morning and quit. Didn't even bother giving notice. She wasn't happy, said I was leaving them short-staffed, but I didn't care. I couldn't go back there.

The weird thing is, a few weeks later, I ran into one of the day shift workers at a coffee shop. She told me they'd had trouble keeping anyone on nights since I left. Said people kept quitting after their first shift, all of them saying the same thing about feeling watched, about hearing footsteps in empty aisles.

I didn't tell her what I'd seen. Didn't tell her about the shadows or the lights or that figure. But sometimes, when I can't sleep, I think about it. About what would have happened if I'd stayed just a few seconds longer. If I'd seen its face.

I don't work night shifts anymore. Don't even like being in stores close to closing time.

Chapter Ten

The Man at the Window

"The camera didn't catch it, but I did." ~ Amanda, Colorado

It started with the dreams. Or at least, I thought they were dreams.

I kept waking up in the middle of the night, heart pounding, my skin cold and damp. I never remembered what I had been dreaming about, just that I'd come out of sleep feeling... exposed. Like something was wrong or someone was watching me.

At first, I did what anyone would do...I explained it away. Stress, maybe. Too much time scrolling my phone before bed. A bad sleeping position. There was no reason to feel this way. My house was secure. I checked the locks every night before going to bed. The windows were closed and locked. The blinds were drawn. There was no way anyone could be watching me.

And yet... the feeling didn't go away.

It didn't happen every night, but often enough that I started dreading waking up in the dark. Some nights, I'd roll over and squeeze my eyes shut, trying to force myself back to sleep. Other nights, I'd reach for my phone, just to see the familiar glow of the screen, something normal to ground me.

Nothing in my house was ever out of place. The doors stayed locked. I had no reason to be afraid.

So I told myself it was all in my head. And for a while... I believed it.

One morning, I woke up and noticed my bedroom curtains were slightly open. I knew I had closed them the night before. I was sure of it. I got up, pulled them shut again, and tried not to think about it. Maybe I hadn't closed them as tightly as I thought.

Then the motion sensor light started acting up. At first, it wasn't that weird, just flicking on randomly, like it was picking up movement. I figured it was an animal. A raccoon, a stray cat, something like that. But every time I checked, there was nothing there.

A few nights later, I was lying in bed, just about to drift off, when I heard something outside. A faint noise, like someone moving through the grass. I stayed as still as possible, listening, barely breathing. The sound came again. I sat up and turned toward the window.

I checked, the yard was empty.

Then, a few days later, my neighbor mentioned something in passing that made my skin crawl.

"Did you have someone over the other night?" she asked as we stood by the mailbox.

I frowned. "No... why?"

She shrugged. "I thought I saw someone walking near your house really late. Like, two in the morning."

I forced a laugh. "Probably just someone passing by."

She nodded and changed the subject. But the whole time, I kept thinking about it.

My street is a dead end.

No one just passes by.

I woke up gasping, heart beating so hard it hurt.

The room was silent, the kind of silence that felt too deep, too unnatural. I wasn't sure what had woken me, but the second my eyes opened, I felt it—this awful, overwhelming sense that I wasn't alone. That someone was watching me.

I didn't want to look. Every nerve in my body told me to squeeze my eyes shut, to stay still, to pretend I was asleep. But I couldn't. I turned my head toward the window.

And there he was.

Just for a second. A shadow, standing outside. Still. Watching.

Then, before my brain could even process what I was seeing, he was gone.

I shot up and I turned on every light I could reach, then forced myself to check the doors, the windows. Everything was locked.

I stood there for a long time, breathing hard. There was no one there now.

It had to be a dream. Or a shadow from the streetlights. Or… something.

I climbed back into bed, but I didn't sleep again that night.

I woke up gasping, heart beating so hard it hurt. The next day, I bought a security camera.

It was small, barely noticeable, and I positioned it so it pointed directly at my bedroom window. If someone had been out there, I wanted proof. More than that, I wanted reassurance… something to show me there was nothing to be afraid of.

For the first few nights, the footage was boring. Just still images of my backyard, the occasional sway of trees in the wind. No figures. No movement. But I still woke up feeling watched.

Then one morning, I noticed my curtains were open wider than I remembered leaving them again.

I checked the footage, expecting to see something, anything… but there was nothing. No movement. No sign that the curtains had been touched.

The only thing unusual was the motion sensor light. Sometime around 3 a.m., it flicked on. But there was no figure. No animal. Just the empty yard, bathed in artificial light for a few minutes before going dark again.

I stared at the screen, trying to make sense of it. The camera didn't show anything.

I woke up again. Not startled this time… just suddenly awake.

I didn't move. I didn't turn toward the window. Instead, I reached for my phone, fingers unsteady as I opened the live feed from the security camera.

And there he was.

A figure, standing completely still outside my window. Not moving. Not shifting. Just watching.

A wave of cold ran through me, and for a long moment, I couldn't think. My mind was screaming at me to look... to turn my head, to see if he was really there... but I was afraid. Because if I looked... what if he was closer?

Finally, I forced myself to move. I turned my head toward the window.

Nothing. Just the empty yard, the faint outline of trees in the dark.

I swallowed hard and looked back at my phone. The figure was still there.

I watched the feed, my pulse pounding, waiting for him to move. But he didn't. He just stood there, motionless. And then, without a sound, without a single step... he was gone.

Not walked away. Just... gone.

I don't remember how I managed to call the police with my hands shaking so badly, but I did. The officers arrived fast, sweeping the yard with flashlights, checking every corner, every possible hiding spot.

They found nothing.

No footprints. No disturbances. No sign that anyone had ever been there.

I showed them the video, desperate for them to see what I had seen. But when they played it back, the footage was normal. Empty. No figure. No proof.

They were kind about it, told me it was probably a trick of the light, maybe an animal setting off the motion sensor. They suggested I get some rest.

But I knew better.

I never saw him again after that night. Not in my window, not on the camera. But the feeling never left. That awful sense of being watched.

Every night before bed, I check the locks. I close the curtains tightly.

And I wonder if he's still out there.

CHAPTER ELEVEN

The Victorian Renovation

"I've worked in tons of old houses, but that one didn't want to be fixed." ~ Michael, New Jersey

I never used to believe in any of this supernatural stuff. I mean, I'm a contractor - I deal with concrete things, you know? Wood and nails and drywall. Real stuff you can touch. Maybe you can tell me what you think.

It was supposed to be a straightforward job. Just updating the kitchen and bathrooms, maybe fixing some old wiring. The kind of work I'd done a hundred times before. But the moment I walked through that front door with my tools, something felt different. Like the air itself was thick with something I couldn't quite explain.

The house had been empty for a while - probably two years, the realtor said. The new owners were this young couple who'd gotten it for a steal, probably because it needed so much work. They weren't living there yet, wanted the renovations done first, which meant I had the place to myself during the days.

At first, everything was normal. Well, as normal as it gets in these old houses. You know how they are - creaky floorboards, settling noises, weird drafts. I started in the kitchen, tearing out those ancient cabinets, pulling up three layers of linoleum to get to the original hardwood underneath. Basic stuff.

But then my tools started moving.

Not like, flying across the room or anything. Just not being where I left them. I'd put my hammer down on the counter, turn to grab something else, and when I looked back, it would be on the other side of the room. Or I'd set my level down, and a minute later it would be somewhere completely different.

I figured I was just being forgetful. When you're focused on work, sometimes you do things without thinking. But after the third or fourth time, I started paying more attention. Started making mental notes of exactly where I put things.

Didn't matter. They still moved.

Then the temperature thing started. You'd walk through these sudden cold spots - like, freezing cold, even though it was middle of summer and the AC wasn't even running yet. They weren't random either. They were always in the same places: the bottom of the stairs, the corner of the living room, and right in front of this one-bedroom door upstairs.

Then one morning, I came in and found all my tools, every single one I'd left there overnight, lined up perfectly straight along the kitchen counter. Not scattered where I'd left them after cleaning up. Not tossed in my toolbox. Just... lined up. Perfectly. Like someone had spent time arranging them.

That's when the footsteps started.

I was upstairs, measuring for the new bathroom vanity, when I heard them. Clear as day - someone walking around downstairs. Heavy steps, like work boots on hardwood. I figured maybe the owners had stopped by, so I called out. No answer. Just more footsteps, moving from the kitchen to the living room.

I went downstairs to check. Nobody there. Every door still locked, every window closed. But the footsteps... they kept going. Now they were upstairs, right above me, moving across the bedroom I'd just left.

I could feel my heart beating out of my chest so hard I could feel it in my throat. I'm not ashamed to admit it, I got out of there pretty fast that day. Yeah, old house make noises... but this was not normal.

But the next day... man, I wish I'd quit right then.

I was in the kitchen again, installing the new cabinets, when I heard someone clear their throat. Right behind me. Like, right there.

Nothing. Nobody there. Just that heavy feeling in the air, stronger than ever.

Then I saw the handprint on the window.

It was on the inside of the glass, like someone had pressed their palm against it. I had looked out that window several times before, like 10 minutes before even, it was not there before. And this handprint... it was huge. Way bigger than mine. Way bigger than any normal person's should be.

As I stood there staring at it, trying to make sense of what I was seeing, it just... faded away. Like it was evaporating.

That's when I noticed how quiet it was. You know how old houses always have some kind of noise - pipes creaking, wood settling, something? Yeah, this was different. This was complete silence. The kind that feels like it's pressing against your ears.

And then I heard it. A voice. Real quiet, like someone talking from another room, but clear enough that I could make out the words:

"You need to leave."

I've never packed up my tools so fast in my life. I was halfway to my truck before you knew it.

That's when I looked up at the second-floor window.

There was someone standing there. Just... watching me. Tall - too tall for the window frame. Dark. And their face... God, I still have trouble sleeping when I think about their face.

I called the owners that night, made up some excuse about a family emergency. Said I couldn't finish the job. They weren't happy, but I didn't care. Some things aren't worth any amount of money.

A few weeks later, I ran into their realtor while out and about. Turns out they never did finish those renovations. Three other contractors started the job. None of them finished it. The couple ended up selling the house for even less than they paid.

I still do renovations. Still work on old houses. But now? I pay attention to that feeling you get when you first walk in. That heaviness in the air. And if I feel it? I don't care how good the money is. I walk away.

Chapter Twelve
The Guest Room

"I used to think I was just a kid that was afraid of the dark. Now I know better." ~ Anonymous, North Carolina

I never liked the guest room at my aunt's house. Even as a kid, it made me uneasy.

Nothing ever happened, exactly. But whenever I had to sleep there, I felt scared, like something was there. Sometimes, I'd convince myself I'd heard something in the middle of the night... but by morning, it never seemed like a big deal. Just a kid getting spooked in the dark. I never told anyone about it because I didn't really have anything to tell. There were no shadows moving in the corners, no hands reaching out from under the bed. Just that strange feeling I could never explain.

Now, years later, I was back for a visit, and my aunt didn't hesitate to offer me the same room. I almost made an excuse to turn it down. Almost. But I felt ridiculous. It was just a room.

So, I said yes.

The moment I stepped inside, though, the feeling came back.

It looked normal. The bed was neatly made, the furniture the same as I remembered. The same antique dresser against the far wall, the same heavy curtains framing the window. There was a large wooden closet in the corner, its doors shut tight like always. Nothing about it had changed.

I stood there a moment longer than I should have, just taking it in. It felt like the space had been left untouched for a long time. I told myself I was being ridiculous letting childhood fears worry me, and set my bag down by the dresser, doing my best to ignore the way my skin prickled as I turned my back on the room.

I ignored it. I was an adult now. I wasn't going to let an old childhood fear mess with me.

Later that evening, as my aunt and I sat in the living room catching up, she mentioned something offhandedly that made me pause.

"You know, no one ever seems to sleep well in that room," she said with a small laugh. "Strange, isn't it?"

I forced a smile and nodded, but inside, my mind was racing.

I almost asked her what she meant, but something held me back. Maybe I didn't want to hear the answer. Instead, I just made a joke about old houses making weird noises, and she let it go.

When I went back to the guest room later that night, I noticed it right away... it was colder than the rest of the house. Not freezing, just... different than you'd expect, even though the vents were open and the heater was running like normal.

Still, I shook it off and got ready for bed. But as I settled in, the unease only grew. The room felt different at night. More aware. The weight of the air around me made it hard to relax, and every time I shifted under the blankets, I found myself listening, waiting. For what, I wasn't sure.

I told myself it was just in my head and eventually drifted off, but at some point, I woke up. The room was silent, but it didn't feel right.

I turned over, half-asleep, expecting to see nothing out of the ordinary. And for the most part, I didn't. But then I noticed the bedroom door.

It was open.

Just an inch or so, barely noticeable.

I knew I had closed it before bed.

And yet, here it was... open just enough for someone to stand on the other side, watching.

That first night, I convinced myself I had imagined the door being open. Maybe I hadn't latched it all the way. Maybe a draft moved it.

The next night, I woke up again.

The room was still, dimly lit by the glow of the hallway nightlight my aunt always kept on. Everything looked the same, but something felt different.

Then I saw it.

The door was open. That's why the hallway nightlight was lighting the room. The door was open again.

Wider this time.

I sat up slowly, staring at it, waiting for some kind of explanation to come to me. Nothing did.

I threw off the blankets, walked to the doorway, and peeked into the hall. It was empty. No sound, no movement. My aunt's door was shut, the house as silent as it should have been.

I closed the door again, pressing against it a little harder this time, making sure to hear it latch.

When I got back into bed, I pulled the covers up to my chin and faced the door, watching it until I finally drifted off.

Over the next few nights, it got worse.

One morning, I woke up to find my blankets pulled slightly down, bunched near my waist like they had been tugged in the night. I was a restless sleeper, but something about it didn't sit right with me. That's never happened before.

Then the closet door.

I never opened it, because I had no reason to. But one morning, it was open. Just enough to see inside.

I tried to explain it away. Maybe I hadn't noticed it before. Maybe it had been open all along. But it was getting harder to ignore the way the unease clung to me, how it stayed in my mind all day.

And then the dreams started.

I was standing in the room, but I wasn't alone. I couldn't see them, not really, but I knew they were there, standing just behind me, just out of sight. Watching.

Every time I woke up, it was at the same hour. The same creeping dread in my chest.

And then, one night, I heard a whisper.

Faint, almost impossible to make out.

I held my breath, straining to listen.

It stopped immediately.

As if it knew I was awake.

The last night, I woke up differently. Not slowly, not groggy—just wide awake, instantly alert. And I couldn't move, like I physically could not move.

I tried to sit up, but my body wouldn't respond. My arms, my legs... nothing. I could only breathe, and even that felt shallow, like something was pressing down on me.

I started to panic. My eyes darted around the room, desperate to find something, anything, that made sense. And then in the corner of the room, I saw that something stood in the dim light. A shape, just barely darker than the shadows around it. Unmoving.

I couldn't blink. Couldn't look away. My whole body screamed to react, to fight, to run! But I was trapped in place, forced to stare at that figure standing so impossibly still.

Seconds dragged. Maybe minutes. My vision blurred and I was feeling pure terror. And then... it faded.

Just... slowly thinned out, dissolving into the darkness like it had never been there at all.

And just like that, I could move again.

I threw myself out of bed, switched on every light, and sat there, shaking, waiting for morning.

The next day, I told my aunt I wouldn't be sleeping in that room again.

She didn't look surprised. She hesitated, then said, "Your uncle always hated that room too. He swore he saw someone standing there at night."

That was all she said, like it wasn't something worth questioning. Like it was just a fact of the house.

I never slept in that room again. In fact, every time I visit now, I never spend the night. And I make sure not to look toward the guest room door.

Chapter Thirteen

The Watcher in the Parking Lot

"I thought I was just being paranoid." ~ Anonymous, Illinois

Working nights changes how you see the world. Everything feels different in the middle of the night... emptier, quieter, like you're moving through a place that wasn't meant for people. I got used to it, mostly. Had to, working the night shift at the hospital. But what happened in that parking lot... that's something I'll never get used to.

I've been a nurse for six years now. Night shift wasn't my first choice, but the pay was better, and honestly, I liked the quiet. Less chaos, more time with patients. The hospital is different at night. Hallways empty except for staff, monitors beeping in darkened rooms, that kind of hushed atmosphere that settles over everything.

The parking lot, though. That's where it started.

It's a big lot, stretches around three sides of the hospital. Staff parking is in the back, under these old sodium lights that cast everything in an ugly yellow glow. Most nights there'd only be maybe ten cars scattered across the whole section... just us night shifters and the occasional visitor.

I'd been working nights for almost a year when I first saw him.

It was a Tuesday, I think. Just another normal shift. I was walking to my car around 5:30 AM, dead on my feet after a rough night in the ICU. That's when I noticed someone standing in the far corner of the lot, where the light from the last lamp post barely reaches.

Just a man, standing perfectly still, facing the hospital. I figured he was a visitor, maybe someone who'd gotten bad news and needed a moment alone. We see that sometimes. People who step outside to process things, to breathe. So, I didn't think much of it.

But the next night, he was there again. Same spot. Same position. Same dark coat.

By the third night, something started nagging at me. Who stands in exactly the same spot, night after night, without moving? I mean, I'd watched him for nearly ten minutes that first morning, and he hadn't shifted his weight, hadn't looked around, hadn't done any of those little movements people naturally make.

I mentioned it to one of the other nurses, trying to play it off as a joke. "Think I've got a secret admirer in the parking lot."

She laughed. "Maybe it's one of those patient family members who fell in love with their nurse. Happens all the time in movies, right?"

But it didn't feel romantic. It felt... stalkerish.

I started parking closer to the entrance after that. Started walking faster to my car, keeping my keys ready in my hand. But every morning, I could feel him watching me. Even when I tried not to look in that direction, I knew he was there. Knew he was watching.

After a couple of weeks of this, I couldn't take it anymore. I went to security, found the security guard at the front desk. He's been there forever, knows everyone, sees everything. I tried to sound casual when I asked him about the man in the parking lot.

"Which man?" he asked, looking up from his crossword puzzle.

I described what I'd been seeing... the dark coat, the way he never moved, how he was there every single morning in the exact same spot. The guard's expression changed, just slightly, but enough to make my stomach tighten.

"Let's check the cameras," he said, setting aside his puzzle.

The security office was small, walls lined with monitors showing different areas of the hospital. Rick pulled up the feed from the back lot, scrolling through footage from the past few mornings.

"There," I said, pointing to the screen. "He stands right there. I can see him out the window now."

He leaned forward, squinting at the monitor. "Where?"

"He's out there, by the last light post. He's wearing a dark coat."

He looked at me, then back at the screen. "There's no one there."

My blood ran cold. "What do you mean? He's standing right there. I can see him from the window."

He got up and walked to the window overlooking the lot. I followed. The man was still there, exactly where he'd been every morning. Standing perfectly still, facing the hospital.

"I don't see anyone," he said quietly.

I stared at him, then back at the lot. The man hadn't moved. Hadn't changed. Was still watching.

That's when the real fear started. Was I the only one that could see him? Why me?

I began rushing to my car every morning, refusing to look toward that corner of the lot. But sometimes I'd catch glimpses in my peripheral vision. And after a while, he seemed to be getting closer. Like he'd taken a few steps forward while I wasn't watching.

The dreams started soon after. I'd wake up in the middle of the day, drenched in sweat, certain he was standing at the foot of my bed. But when I opened my eyes, there was nothing. Just that lingering feeling of being watched.

I started asking the guard to walk me to my car. He never complained, but he also never saw what I saw. Every morning, I'd watch his face as we walked across the lot, looking for any sign that he finally noticed the man. But he never did.

One night, after a particularly bad shift, I finally asked him: "Has anyone else ever reported seeing something strange in the parking lot?"

He was quiet for a long moment. "Not exactly," he said finally. "But..."

"But what?"

He sighed, looking uncomfortable. "Look, I've worked here a long time. These old hospitals, they collect stories. Things people see late at night, when they're alone. Things that don't show up on cameras."

"What kind of things?"

"I probably shouldn't say more." He wouldn't meet my eyes. "I've heard stories over the years, but I've never seen anything, okay?"

That morning, something was different. I stepped out of the hospital, and for the first time in weeks, the man wasn't in his usual spot. For a split second, relief flooded through me.

Then I saw him.

He was standing by the hospital entrance. Right where I needed to walk to reach my car.

I was dumbfounded. In all these weeks, he'd never been this close. I could see details now, how his coat seemed to absorb the light around it, how his face was somehow both there and not there, if that makes any sense. I don't know how else to describe it.

I ran. Didn't even try to be subtle about it. Just sprinted to my car, fumbled with my keys, threw myself inside, and locked the doors. As I backed out of my spot, I looked in my rearview mirror.

He was watching me leave. Standing just at the edge of the light, perfectly still.

After that, I switched to day shift the next week, and haven't seen him since.

I still work at the same hospital. Still park in that back lot, even though I'm on days now. Sometimes new nurses on night shift mention feeling watched, and I see the security guard giving them the same look he gave me. That mix of concern and resignation, like he knows exactly what they're talking about but can't, or won't, say more.

I want to warn them. Want to tell them to look behind them, to watch the shadows, to never assume they're alone just because they can't see anyone else around.

But I don't. Because what could I say? That there's something in the parking lot that only some people can see?

So if you're reading this, and you work nights, and you ever feel like you're being watched... don't look. Don't ever look. Because once you see him, he sees you too.

And he never stops watching.

CHAPTER FOURTEEN

The Room with the Blue Door

"I wish I had listened and stayed away." ~ Danny, Virginia

When I was a kid, my grandparents' house always felt a little strange to me. It wasn't the house itself. It was cozy, warm, the kind of place where you'd expect to feel safe. But there was one part of it that never sat right with me. The hallway upstairs, the one that led to the guest rooms and my grandparents' bedroom, had a door at the very end. It was faded blue, the paint chipped around the edges like it had been there forever.

I was never allowed inside.

No one ever told me why.

It was just understood. If I asked about it, my grandmother would simply say, "That room stays closed." My grandfather, on the other hand, wouldn't say anything at all.

I wasn't a particularly brave kid, so I never pushed the issue. But every time I played upstairs, I'd find myself stopping in front of that door, staring at it. There was something about it that gave me chills. The rest of the house smelled like old books and my grandmother's cooking, but the hallway by that door smelled different, like dust and something else I couldn't place.

I remember pressing my hand against the wood once, just to see if I could feel anything. The door was always cool. Sometimes, if I stood there long enough, I'd swear I felt the faintest draft coming from underneath it.

It wasn't just me.

I didn't realize it at the time, but no one in my family spent much time near that end of the hallway. They never said it outright, but looking back, I can see it. The way my grandmother moved quickly past the door without glancing at it. The way my grandfather would hesitate for just a second before walking by, like he was listening for something.

We never talked about it. But little things happened.

Whenever I passed by the door, I felt like I wasn't alone in that hallway. The sensation would hit me out of nowhere, like the moment I stepped too close.

Even in the dead of summer, that part of the house was always colder. The rest of the upstairs could be stifling, but the space around the blue door? It felt like stepping into a basement.

And then there were the sounds.

Some nights, when I stayed over, I'd hear them. Soft, too quiet to be sure. Faint whispering, like someone was talking just behind the door. Gentle tapping, like fingertips against wood. It never lasted long enough for me to be certain, but it happened often enough that I started sleeping with a pillow over my head.

I asked my grandfather about it once. I remember it so clearly because it was the only time he ever spoke about that room at all.

He didn't look at me when he answered. Just kept reading his newspaper and said, "Some doors are better left closed."

And that was that.

No one ever spoke about it again. It was as if the door wasn't there.

My grandparents had left just before sunset to pick up something from the store... milk, I think. The sky had been clear when they left, nothing unusual about the evening. I was old enough to stay home alone, so I curled up on the couch with the TV on, barely paying attention to the quiet outside.

Then, not long after they were gone, the wind picked up. Dark clouds rolled in fast, rattling the windows as rain started to hammer against the roof.

Then I heard it.

A loud thud from upstairs.

I listened hard. The wind was loud, sure, but this noise had come from inside the house. Something solid, something unmistakable. I turned the volume down on the TV and listened, waiting for another sound.

Nothing. Just the storm outside.

I tried to convince myself it was nothing. But a feeling crept in, a familiar discomfort I hadn't felt since I was little. Slowly, I stood up and made my way toward the stairs, my breath unsteady. As I reached the second floor, my eyes landed on the hallway… and that's when I saw it.

The blue door.

It was open.

Not much. But that door had always been closed. Locked. Untouched.

I sat there, staring, my breath shallow. Every instinct told me to stay put, to wait for my grandparents to come home. But I couldn't look away. I had spent my whole childhood wondering what was behind that door. Now it was open.

And I had to know.

I moved slowly, creeping up the stairs. With each step, my skin prickled, like I was being watched. The closer I got, the stronger that feeling became.

I reached the door and hesitated, my hand hovering near the knob. The room was dark, the sliver of space between the door and the frame not revealing much.

I pushed it open.

The room was empty.

Dust floated inside. It hadn't been entered of cleaned for years. The wooden floor was bare except for a single rocking chair, old and creaking slightly as if it had just been sat in. It faced the door.

The air inside felt stuffy. Still and stale, carrying a scent that reminded me of an attic left shut for too long. My chest tightened as I stepped inside, just far enough for my foot to press into the dust-covered floorboards.

Then a sudden burst of cold air shot past me.

I gasped and stumbled back, heart racing. It felt like something had brushed against me, moved past me. But there was nothing there. Just that chair. Just the dust. Just the silence.

I turned to leave.

The door slammed shut.

I jumped, grabbing the knob and twisting, pulling, but it wouldn't budge. The knob felt ice-cold under my fingers.

I banged on the door. "Let me out!" My voice sounded small in the emptiness.

Then... the door creaked. Not from me pulling it, but on its own. The latch released, and the door drifted open just enough for me to see the hallway.

I didn't stop to question it. I ran. Down the stairs, through the living room, straight to the front door. But the wind was howling outside, rain slamming against the windows so hard I knew there was no way I could go outside. Instead, I turned on all the lights ran back to the couch and covered with my blanket, as if that would protect me from anything.

I didn't talk about the blue door for a long time. Even after that night, after running down the stairs and waiting in the living room with every light on until my grandparents came home, I never told them what happened. It felt like something I wasn't supposed to say out loud.

Years passed, and I grew up. Life moved on. The strange memories from childhood... the ones that didn't make sense... got pushed to the back of my mind. Until I visited my grandmother again, after my grandfather passed away.

The house felt smaller than I remembered. Or maybe I had just gotten bigger. But when I walked through it, I still knew every creaky floorboard, every faded picture on the walls. And when I made my way upstairs, I stopped at the end of the hall without thinking. The blue door was still there. Still closed. Still locked.

At dinner that night, I finally asked.

"Why was that room always locked?"

I expected her to laugh, to wave a hand and tell me I was being dramatic. But she didn't. She set down her fork, and for the first time since I arrived, she looked... uneasy.

"That door was locked for a reason," she said quietly.

I waited, but she didn't say anything else.

"What reason?" I pressed.

She hesitated, then sighed. "Your great-uncle passed away in that room. A long time ago, before you were born. After that, your grandfather kept it shut. He never talked about it, never let anyone use it." Her eyes glanced toward the hallway, just for a second. "He didn't even like us mentioning it."

I felt a chill run through me. "Did something... happen in there?"

She shook her head. "I don't know. He wouldn't say. Just that it needed to stay closed."

Eventually, the house was sold. I never set foot in it again. Not after that conversation. Not after remembering what I had felt that night all those years ago.

But even now, years later, I still dream about the blue door.

Chapter Fifteen
The Woman by the Guardrail

"We thought she needed help." ~ Sarah, New York

They say your instincts can sense danger before your mind catches up. That little voice in your head telling you something isn't right? You should always listen to it. I wish we had that night.

It was late October, and my husband Dan and I were driving back from his sister's wedding in Millbrook. The reception had run long, and we'd stayed to help clean up. By the time we left, it was well after dark. Dan knew a shortcut home through the back roads—mostly farmland and woods, but it would save us some time, and we were beat.

The roads were empty that night. No streetlights, no houses, not even any other cars. Just us and the sound of tires on asphalt. I remember looking at the clock: 11:47 PM. I was tired, half-dozing in the passenger seat, when we came around that bend.

"Dan," I said, suddenly wide awake. "Dan, stop the car."

There was a woman standing by the guardrail. Just... standing there. She was wearing what looked like a light-colored dress, and she was completely still, staring out into the darkness beyond the road. The guardrail next to her was bent and twisted, like something had hit it hard.

"Did you see her?" I asked as we drove past. "We have to go back. She might need help."

Dan didn't answer right away. His hands tightened on the steering wheel. He did trust stopping for strangers. "I don't know, Sarah. If she needed help, wouldn't she have waved us down?"

"Maybe she's hurt. Or in shock." I turned in my seat, trying to see her through the back window, but we'd already rounded another curve. "We can't just leave her out here alone."

He sighed, but I could tell he was worried too. "Okay. But let's be careful."

Dan slowed down and made a u-turn. The whole time, I kept thinking about that woman. Something about the way she was standing... it reminded me of people I'd seen in the ER where I worked. People who were dissociating after trauma, just completely checked out.

The drive back to that spot felt longer than it should have. Maybe because we were both tense. Our headlights swept across empty road, then trees, then the damaged guardrail.

But the woman was gone.

"Stop the car," I said again, but this time my voice was barely a whisper.

Dan pulled over. We sat there for a moment, staring at the empty roadside. There was nowhere she could have gone. On one side was dense forest, on the other a steep drop into darkness.

"Maybe... maybe she walked down the road?" Dan suggested, but we both knew that was impossible. We would have seen her—the road stretched straight ahead for at least half a mile.

I got out of the car before I could talk myself out of it.

"Sarah, wait." Dan was beside me now, holding up his phone as a flashlight. The beam caught the twisted metal of the guardrail, showing deep scrapes. Beyond it was just blackness—a sharp slope dropping away into nothing.

"Hello?" I called out. "Is anyone there? Do you need help?"

No answer.

Then I noticed some flowers. Half-hidden in the tall grass near the guardrail was a small bouquet. They were fresh, with a purple ribbon tied around them.

"Dan," I said, my stomach clenching. "Call the police."

He was already dialing. I heard him trying to explain to the dispatcher what we'd seen, where we were. They wanted us to stay until an officer could arrive.

We got back in the car, but left the headlights on, pointing at the guardrail. Neither of us spoke. I kept watching that spot where she had been standing, trying to make sense of what we'd seen. The image was burned into my mind: her rigid posture, the way she'd been staring into space, her dress so pale it almost glowed in our headlights.

After what felt like hours but was probably only twenty minutes, we saw blue and red lights approaching. The patrol car pulled up behind us, and an officer got out.

We told him everything—the woman, how she'd vanished. He listened carefully, writing in his notepad, but something about his expression made my skin crawl. Like he wasn't surprised.

He walked over to the guardrail with his flashlight, checking the area carefully. Then he came back to us, flipping his notepad closed.

"This is a bad stretch of road," he said finally. "Lots of accidents over the years. The most recent was just yesterday." He paused, looking at the guardrail. "Young woman lost control in the rain. By the time we got here..." He shook his head. "The flowers are from her family."

I felt the blood drain from my face. Dan's hand found mine, squeezing hard.

"That's impossible," I whispered, but even as I said it, I knew. The pale dress. The way she stood so still. The complete silence.

The officer gave us a long look. "Drive safe," he said quietly. "Especially at night." He turned and walked back to his car without another word.

We watched his taillights disappear around the curve. Neither of us moved.

"Sarah," Dan said finally, his voice rough. "What did we see?"

I didn't answer. I couldn't.

Dan started the car and pulled away.

That was five years ago. We never take that road anymore, even in daylight. We've never talked about what happened, not really. What could we say? That we saw a ghost? That she was still there, trapped in her last moments?

But sometimes, when I'm driving at night and I see someone on the side of the road, I don't stop. Not anymore.

I still think about her, though. I wonder if she's still there, standing by that broken guardrail, staring into the darkness. I wonder if other drivers see her too. If they stop, like we did, only to find empty air and fresh flowers.

I mentioned this once to Dan, and he just got quiet. Really quiet. Then he told me something he'd never said before. That night, when we were pulling away? He looked in the rearview mirror. And for just a second, he saw her watching us leave. Not by the guardrail anymore, but in the middle of the road.

Chapter Sixteen

The Apartment Next Door

"There were voices were coming from next door." ~ Anonymous, Texas

I never wanted to believe in ghosts. I'm not that kind of person. I like facts, things I can prove. Even now, I catch myself trying to find some rational explanation for what happened in that apartment. But I can't. I've tried.

This was about a year ago, right after my ex and I split up. Five years together, then suddenly I'm living out of boxes, trying to find somewhere I can afford on my own. The apartment wasn't much, one of those older complexes from the '70s, all brick and beige carpet, but it was clean and quiet. That's all I needed.

The landlord, seemed decent enough. Showed me around, explained about the window unit AC, pointed out the sticky spot on the kitchen floor he was planning to fix. Standard stuff. When I asked about neighbors, he mentioned the unit next door was empty.

"Been vacant a few months," he said. "Previous tenant moved out of state for work."

I remember thinking that was perfect. One less person to deal with while I got my life sorted out.

The first week was kind of nice. Unpacking kept my mind off things. I set up my desk by the window, hung some pictures, tried to make it feel like home. During the day, I could hear kids playing in the courtyard, cars in the parking lot, normal apartment sounds. But at night, it was so quiet I could hear the refrigerator humming from across the room.

That's probably why I noticed the voices.

It was maybe my fourth or fifth night there. I was drifting off to sleep when I heard.... just a murmur, like someone talking in low tones on the other side of the wall. Not loud enough to make out words, just a soft rise and fall of voices.

I barely thought about it. Just figured someone had moved in next door without me noticing. I mean, I was at work all day. Easy enough to miss.

But it kept happening. Every night, always just quiet enough that I couldn't quite make out what they were saying. Sometimes it would go on for hours—this constant, gentle murmur of conversation. Sometimes I'd hear other sounds too, like furniture being dragged across the floor or cabinets opening and closing.

I started paying more attention to the unit next door. Never saw lights on. Never heard doors opening or closing. Never caught anyone in the hallway. Just those voices, night after night, seeping through the wall.

Then came the night I heard my name.

I was lying in bed, staring at the ceiling, listening to those muffled voices when suddenly one got clearer. Just for a second. Just long enough to whisper "Daniel" in this weird, echoing way that made my skin crawl.

I sat up, fully awake now. The voices continued, soft and unintelligible again. Without really thinking it through, I knocked on the wall. Three sharp raps.

The voices stopped immediately. It was silent.

Then... one single knock in response.

I didn't sleep much that night.

The next morning, I caught the landlord in the parking lot. I tried to sound casual when I asked about the new tenants next door.

He frowned. "New tenants? That unit's still empty. Nobody's even looked at it this month."

My stomach dropped. "But I hear voices in there. At night. People talking."

His expression changed, just slightly. Like he was choosing his words carefully. "Probably just the TV from the unit above. Sound carries weird in these old buildings."

But I knew what I was hearing. And it wasn't coming from upstairs.

I started keeping a log. The voices usually started around 1 AM, lasting anywhere from a few minutes to several hours. Sometimes they were barely audible. Other times they were clear enough that I could tell there were multiple voices speaking at once, overlapping each other in this strange way.

One night, I pressed my ear against the wall, determined to make out what they were saying. The voices got clearer, but... not normal. They didn't sound like normal conversation anymore. More like dozens of whispers layered on top of each other, speaking words I couldn't quite catch.

I pulled away from the wall, my heart pounding. The voices continued, but now they seemed to be coming from different points along the wall. Like whatever was in there was moving around.

That's when things got worse.

I woke up one night... 3:42 AM according to my phone, to a whisper right next to my ear. Not through the wall. Right there, in my room.

I stay completely still, even holding my breath. The whisper came again, closer this time, like lips right against my ear. I couldn't make out the words, but I could feel the cold breath on my skin.

Then... knock. Knock. Knock.

But it wasn't coming from the wall anymore. It was coming from my headboard. Something was in my room, knocking on my bed.

I bolted up and turned on the lights, ready to fight the intruder. But no one was there... my room was empty. I grabbed my pillow and blanket and ran to the living room. Spent the rest of the night on the couch with every light on, jumping at every little sound.

The next day, I confronted the landlord. Demanded to see inside the empty apartment. He tried to brush me off, but I wouldn't let it go. Finally, he agreed, probably just to shut me up.

The unit was empty. Completely empty. Clean beige carpet, blank walls, not a stick of furniture. No sign anyone had been in there for months.

I walked through every room, looking for... I don't know what. Some evidence of what I'd been hearing. There was nothing. Just empty space and silence.

We were about to leave when I heard it. A soft shuffling sound from the bedroom we'd just checked. Like someone dragging their feet across carpet.

The landlord heard it too. I saw him freeze, keys halfway to the lock.

"Old pipes," he said quickly. "Building settles at weird times."

But I saw the way his hand shook as he locked the door. He knew something.

That night, I lay awake in my living room, staring at my bedroom door. I'd closed it firmly, telling myself whatever was in there couldn't get out. Around 2 AM, the voices started again. But this time, they weren't coming from next door.

They were coming from my bedroom.

I moved out the next day. Broke my lease, lost my deposit, didn't care. The landlord didn't even argue. Just took my keys and looked away when I asked if anyone had ever died in either apartment.

I live in a house now. No shared walls, no empty units next door.

Chapter Seventeen

The Unfinished Call

"It sounded like her." ~ Mark, Pennsylvania

I never used to think twice about answering my phone. Now? Now I keep it face down at night. Keep it on silent when I'm alone. Sometimes I think about getting rid of it entirely, but I know that wouldn't help. Whatever was trying to reach me through those calls, it doesn't need a working phone line anymore.

It started last October. I was driving home from work, just another normal Tuesday evening. Traffic was bad, and I was focused on navigating through the rush hour mess when I noticed the notification light blinking on my phone. Missed call and voicemail from Mom.

That was weird in itself. Mom never calls during work hours unless it's important. She knows my schedule, knows I can't usually answer until after five. So when I saw her name, my stomach did this little flip. Something must be wrong.

I pulled into a gas station and played the voicemail. It was short—just her voice saying my name, "Mark?" But the way she said it... I can still hear it perfectly. This wavering, worried tone I'd never heard from her before. Then it cut off abruptly, like something had interrupted her.

I called her back immediately, my hands shaking slightly as I held the phone. She picked up on the third ring, sounding completely normal.

"Everything okay?" I asked, trying to keep my voice steady. "I got your voicemail. You sounded worried."

"What voicemail?" She sounded genuinely confused. "I haven't called you today, honey."

I checked my call log. Nothing. No incoming call, no missed call notification. But the voicemail was still there.

"Are you sure?" I pressed. "You left me a message just saying my name. It sounded urgent."

She laughed. "Must be a crossed line or something. I've been in meetings all afternoon, didn't even have my phone with me."

I tried to laugh it off too, but that was really weird and it didn't make sense. I played the voicemail again after we hung up. It was definitely Mom's voice. I'd know it anywhere. But now, listening more carefully, I noticed something else—this weird static in the background, like interference on the line.

I saved the voicemail. Don't know why, really. Just had this feeling I should keep it.

That night, I couldn't sleep. Kept thinking about that message, about the way Mom's voice had sounded. Around 2 AM, I got up and played it again, this time with headphones in so I could hear it clearly.

The static wasn't just static. There was something underneath it—this soft, rhythmic sound. Like breathing. But not normal breathing. More like when someone's trying to breathe very quietly, trying not to be heard.

And the way Mom's voice cut off... it wasn't like a normal disconnect. It was too sudden, too sharp. Like something had stopped her mid-word.

I called her again the next morning, trying to sound casual. "You're absolutely sure you didn't try to call me yesterday? Maybe pocket dial or something?"

"Mark, honey, are you okay?" Now she sounded worried for real. "I told you, I didn't have my phone. It was in my desk all afternoon while I was in meetings."

I forced a laugh. "Yeah, sorry. Just being weird, I guess."

But I couldn't shake it. Something about that voicemail kept nagging at me.

A few days later, Mom called—for real this time. Her voice was shaky.

"I had the strangest dream about you last night," she said without preamble. "You were calling for help, but I couldn't find you. You sounded so scared..."

My blood went cold. "What do you mean?"

"I don't know, exactly. Just... you kept calling my name, but every time I tried to reach you, you seemed further away. And there was this weird noise in the background, like..."

"Like static?" My voice came out barely above a whisper.

She was quiet for a long moment. "Yes. How did you know?"

I was about to tell her about the voicemail when my phone buzzed—another call coming in. From her number.

"Mom," I said slowly, "are you calling me from another phone right now?"

"No, why?"

I stared at the incoming call notification. "Because you're calling me right now. I'm looking at your number."

She made a confused sound. "That's impossible. I'm on my cell, talking to you."

My hands were trembling as I pulled the phone away from my ear to look at the screen. The incoming call was still there, her number clearly displayed.

"I'm going to put you on hold for a second," I said. "Just... just wait."

I switched to the other line. "Hello?"

Static. Just static, and then... a whisper. My name, in a voice that sounded almost like Mom's, but wrong somehow. Distorted. Like someone trying to speak underwater.

I hung up fast, switched back to Mom. "Did you hear anything just now? Any clicking or static?"

"No, nothing. Mark, you're scaring me. What's going on?"

I checked my call log. Just the one ongoing call with Mom. No record of the second call. No evidence it had happened at all.

That's when I knew I had to show her the voicemail. I drove to her house the next day, trying to think of how to explain what was happening without sounding crazy.

She could tell something was wrong the moment she saw me. "I had another dream," she said as I walked in. "You were calling for help again."

I pulled out my phone. "I need you to listen to something."

I played the voicemail. Mom's face went pale.

"That's not me," she whispered. "I mean, it sounds like me, but... that's not my voice. Something's wrong with it."

She was right. Listening to it now, the voice sounded off. The pitch was slightly wrong, the cadence unnatural. Like something was trying to mimic her voice but couldn't quite get it right.

I deleted the voicemail right there. Mom insisted we both start keeping dream journals, tracking anything unusual. We spent hours talking about it, trying to make sense of what was happening.

For a few weeks, everything was quiet. No strange calls, no weird voicemails. I almost convinced myself it had been some kind of elaborate technical glitch.

Then, one night, just as I was drifting off to sleep, my phone lit up. Mom's number on the screen.

I knew she wouldn't be calling at that hour. I knew I shouldn't answer. But I did.

"Hello?"

Static. Then my own voice came through the speaker, distorted and wrong, saying words I'd never spoken: "Help me find you."

I hung up. Checked the call log. Nothing.

My hands were shaking so bad I could barely type, but I managed to send Mom a text: "Did you just call me?"

Her response came quickly: "No. Why?"

I didn't answer. What could I say? That something was using our voices to talk to each other? That it was getting better at mimicking us?

I keep my phone face down now. Keep it on silent. But sometimes, in those quiet hours before dawn, I swear I can hear it—that soft static, that distorted breathing. Even when the phone is off.

Mom still has those dreams. Says they're getting clearer. She told me she can almost make out what the voice is saying now. Not my voice anymore, she says. Something else, just pretending to be me.

I asked her what it's saying, but she wouldn't tell me. Just made me promise to never answer if her number calls late at night.

I think we both know whatever's reaching through those calls isn't finished. It's learning our voices, learning how to sound like us. And sometimes, when my phone lights up in the middle of the night, I wonder... if I answered, would I hear my own voice? Or would I finally hear what's been hiding behind the static all along?

I don't think I want to know. But I have a feeling I'm going to find out, whether I want to or not.

Chapter Eighteen

The Wrong Reflection

"I'm afraid to look in the mirror." ~ Anonymous, New York

You don't realize how many reflective surfaces there are in the world until you start avoiding them. Windows, mirrors, phone screens, puddles... they're everywhere. Most people don't think twice about them. But I do. I have to. Because sometimes what I see looking back isn't quite... me.

It started three years ago. I was walking home from work, taking my usual route down Mason Street. Nothing special about that day, just tired after a long shift at the office, thinking about what I'd make for dinner. I barely noticed the clothing store window as I passed it. You know how it is when you walk the same path every day... your mind wanders, you stop really seeing things.

But something made me look. Just a quick glance, the kind you do without thinking. And for a split second, just the tiniest fraction of a moment, my reflection was facing the wrong way.

I stopped dead in my tracks. When I looked again, everything was normal. Just me, staring wide-eyed at myself in the window, while other pedestrians moved around me on the sidewalk.

I told myself I was just tired. That my eyes were playing tricks on me after staring at spreadsheets all day. I mean, that makes sense, right? Reflections don't move on their own. They can't.

Over the next few days, I kept catching myself looking at reflective surfaces. Not intentionally... more like this weird compulsion I couldn't control. Every window I passed, every mirror, I had to check. Just to make sure everything was normal.

The bathroom mirror at work started to freak me out. I'd stand there washing my hands, watching my reflection a bit too long, waiting to see if something would change. My coworker caught me doing it once.

"You okay?" she asked, giving me an odd look.

I laughed it off. "Yeah, just... checking my makeup."

But I wasn't. I was watching how my reflection moved, trying to convince myself that its movements perfectly matched my own. That there wasn't a slight delay, a tiny hesitation before it followed me.

I started having this recurring dream. I'd be standing in front of a mirror, but my reflection would just... stand there. Not moving. Not blinking. Just watching me. I'd wake up, immediately checking the mirror on my dresser to make sure everything was normal.

Then came one morning at the bus stop. I was running late, anxiously checking the time on my phone, when I happened to glance at my reflection in the glass shelter. Something was wrong. The angle was off, like my shoulders weren't quite aligned with my actual position. Like my reflection was standing just slightly different than I was.

My stomach lurched. I turned away quickly, then forced myself to look back. Everything appeared normal, but that experience stayed with me all day.

That's when I started actively avoiding reflections. I'd keep my eyes straight ahead when passing store windows. I'd use my phone without looking at the dark screen. I'd wash my hands in the bathroom without glancing up at the mirror.

But you can't avoid your own reflection forever. It's like trying not to think about something... the more you try, the more it consumes you.

One evening, walking home, I passed a parked car. I wasn't going to look. I really wasn't. But something in my peripheral vision caught my attention. My reflection in the car window seemed to be moving just a fraction of a second too late, like slightly out of sync.

I stopped. Turned to look directly at it. And of course, everything looked normal. But I knew what I'd seen. That delay. That wrong movement.

When I got home, I draped a scarf over my bathroom mirror. Just for the night, I told myself. Just until I could get some sleep and stop being so paranoid.

But it wasn't paranoia.

A week later, I was walking past that same store window where it all started. I'd been avoiding that street, taking detours around it, but that day I decided enough was enough. I was being ridiculous. I kept my eyes straight ahead, determined not to look.

But at the last second, something made me turn my head. Just slightly. Just enough to see.

My reflection was facing the opposite direction. Just... standing there, showing me the back of its head.

Other people on the sidewalk gave me strange looks as I staggered away from the window. When I looked back, my reflection was normal again, mirroring my terrified expression perfectly.

I ran home. Covered every mirror in my apartment with towels. Turned my phone face-down. Drew all the curtains so I wouldn't catch my reflection in the windows after dark.

The next day, I called in sick to work. Spent hours online, searching for anyone who might have experienced something similar. Found a few forum posts, some Reddit threads... people describing reflections that moved wrong, that didn't quite match their movements. Most of the responses dismissed them as tired, stressed, imagining things.

But I know what I saw.

I changed my route to work. Avoided the bathroom at work when other people weren't around. Stopped wearing makeup because I couldn't bear to look in a mirror long enough to apply it.

I tried to tell my sister about it once. Got halfway through explaining before I saw the look on her face... that mixture of concern and skepticism that made me swallow the rest of my story and laugh it off.

That was a year ago. I've gotten rid of most of the mirrors in my apartment now. Kept one small one in the bathroom, but it stays covered unless I absolutely need it. I've learned to do my hair by touch, to trust that my clothes match without checking my reflection.

Some days are better than others. Some days I almost convince myself I imagined the whole thing. That I'm just stressed, just tired, just letting my imagination run wild.

But then I'll catch something. A flicker in a window as I pass. A movement that doesn't quite match my own. A glimpse of myself turning away when I'm standing still.

I don't know what's happening to me. I don't know if my reflection is becoming something else, or if something else is replacing my reflection. All I know is that what I see in mirrors isn't always me.

Chapter Nineteen
The Car in the Ditch

"Your not the first." ~ Anonymous, Oregon

I never used to mind driving at night. Actually, I preferred it. But that changed after what happened on Route 23. Now I stick to daylight hours whenever I can. When people ask why, I usually make up some excuse about being tired or having bad night vision. The truth? They wouldn't believe me. Sometimes I barely believe it myself.

It was about two years ago. I was driving back from visiting my brother in Cedar Grove, taking the old highway instead of the interstate. It was pushing midnight, but I knew these roads well. I'd made this drive dozens of times.

The night was clear, the stars were bright. No moon though, which made the darkness between towns feel deeper somehow.

I hadn't seen another car for miles when I came around that bend. At first, all I saw were headlights, dim and tilted at a weird angle. Then the rest came into view... a car in the ditch, its front end smashed against a tree. The sight made my stomach drop. Out here, with hardly any traffic, a crash could be serious trouble.

I pulled over.

I sat there for a moment, engine idling. The crash didn't look fresh—no smoke, no scattered debris. Wouldn't someone else have stopped by now? But those headlights were still on. Someone had to be around.

When I stepped out of my car. I left my engine running, headlights pointed toward the wreck, and walked closer.

It was a blue sedan, probably only a few years old. The driver's side door hung open, creaking softly in the wind. I approached carefully, calling out, "Hello? Anyone here? Do you need help?"

No response. Just that endless silence.

I reached the car and peered inside. Empty. The airbags had deployed, and there were cracks in the windshield spreading out like a spider's web. The seats were covered in tiny shards of glass. But no blood, no signs of anyone being hurt.

I pulled out my phone, relieved to see I had one bar of service. The 911 dispatcher answered quickly, and I explained what I'd found. She told me to stay put, that an officer was already nearby and would be there in a few minutes.

I paced a bit, trying to stay warm. I was about to get back in my car when something made me turn around.

There was someone in the driver's seat.

My heart slammed against my ribs. I hadn't heard anyone approach, hadn't heard a door move. But there they were... just a dark shape, slumped forward over the steering wheel.

I rushed forward, already reaching for my phone. "Hey! Are you okay?"

The seat was empty.

I stumbled backward, searching the area, but there was no one. No footprints in the soft ground, no sound of someone running away. Just the empty car with its dim headlights and that awful silence.

Red and blue lights appeared in the distance, and I've never been so relieved to see a police car. The officer walked over. He listened calmly as I told him everything... finding the car, seeing the figure, how it vanished.

When I finished, he nodded slowly and walked to the wreck. His flashlight played over the crumpled metal, the shattered glass. Then he turned back to me with an expression I couldn't read.

"This accident happened yesterday," he said quietly. "Young guy fell asleep at the wheel. He was dead when we found him."

The cold seemed to sink straight into my bones. "But... but I saw someone in there. Just now."

The officer was quiet for a long moment. "You're not the first," he said finally. "Had three calls about this car tonight. Everyone says the same thing—they see someone in the driver's seat, but when they get close..." He shrugged. "Tow truck's coming in the morning to clear it out."

I wanted to ask more questions, but my mouth had gone dry.

"Go on home," he said. "Nothing more you can do here."

I practically ran back to my car. As I pulled away, I couldn't help looking in my rearview mirror. The officer's lights were still flashing.

I looked up the accident report a few days later. I had to know. There it was in black and white—single-car accident, driver pronounced dead at the scene. They'd found him exactly how I saw him, slumped over the steering wheel.

I drive a different route now, even though it adds an extra half hour to the trip. My brother thinks I'm being ridiculous, but he wasn't there. He didn't see what I saw.

Sometimes I wonder about that night. About what would have happened if I'd stayed longer, or if I'd tried to talk to the figure I saw.

CHAPTER TWENTY

The Stranger in the Background

"I don't take pictures anymore." ~ Anonymous, Texas

I used to love taking pictures. You know those friends who always have their phone ready, catching every moment? That was me. My camera roll was full of silly selfies, group shots, random memories I wanted to keep. Now? I haven't taken a photo in over a year. I don't even open the camera app.

It started during a camping trip last fall. Just four of us—me, Ryan, Claire, and John—at this secluded spot near Morrison Lake. We'd been planning it for months, talking about how nice it would be to get away from everything.

The first two days were perfect. Hiking during the day, sitting around the campfire at night, telling stupid stories and laughing at inside jokes. On our last night, we stayed up late, passing around a bottle of whiskey and trying to remember all the ridiculous things we'd done in college.

I remember exactly when I took that first photo. Claire was telling this story, and everyone was cracking up. The firelight made everything look warm and cozy, and I wanted to remember the moment. So I held up my phone, made everyone squeeze together, and snapped a quick selfie.

We glanced at it, laughed at how goofy we looked with the fire casting weird shadows on our faces, and went back to our conversations. Just another photo for the collection. I didn't even really look at it again until the next morning when we were packing up.

I was scrolling through my phone, deleting the blurry shots, when I saw it. In the background, there was... someone. Standing at the edge of the trees, watching us.

"Hey," I said, trying to keep my voice casual. "Was anyone else around last night?"

The others gathered around to look. We were all certain we'd been alone—the nearest campsite was miles away, and we hadn't seen another person all weekend.

"Maybe it's just shadows?" John suggested, but he didn't sound convinced.

We zoomed in on the figure. It was blurry, like photos of movement sometimes are, but it was definitely person-shaped. Just... standing there. Watching our group.

Ryan tried to laugh it off. "Look at that—we've got our own campfire ghost! Probably wanted some of our whiskey."

I saved the photo but tried not to think about it too much. I mean, there had to be a logical explanation, right? Maybe someone was hiking through.

But then it happened again.

We were out celebrating John's birthday a few weeks later. Just a normal night at a bar downtown, taking stupid pictures and having fun. I took a group shot of everyone around the table, not thinking anything of it.

Later that night, I was looking through the photos and I broke out in a sweat. There, by the entrance to the bar, was the same figure. Not similar... identical. The same blurry outline, the same stance, like it was just... watching us.

My hands were shaking as I sent both photos to our group chat. Ryan immediately started trying to explain it away, a coincidence, a trick of the light. But Claire went quiet. Really quiet. When she finally responded, all she said was, "I don't like this."

Then things got worse.

Every time we got together, every photo we took... it was there. Sometimes partially hidden behind things, sometimes standing in plain sight, but always watching. The distance varied, but it was always the same figure, always just blurry enough that you couldn't make out any features.

I started getting paranoid. Found myself checking the background of every picture I took, even ones without the group. Claire refused to be in photos altogether. John became obsessed with trying to figure out what it was, spending hours analyzing the images.

Ryan was the last holdout. He kept insisting there had to be an explanation. Finally, he suggested an experiment.

"Let's take a picture somewhere completely random," he said. "Middle of the day, no one around. If it shows up then, we'll know something's really wrong."

We met at this empty park on the edge of town. Not a soul in sight. Ryan held up his phone, we all squeezed together, and he took the shot.

I'll never forget his face when he looked at that photo. The color just... drained away.

The figure was there. And it was closer than ever before.

We met at my apartment that night to try to make sense of what was happening. Ryan, who'd been so determined to find a logical explanation, finally admitted this wasn't normal. We went through months of old photos from before the camping trip—nothing unusual in any of them.

Whatever this was, it had started that night by the fire.

Then came the night that changed everything.

I woke up at well after midnight. My phone screen was glowing on my nightstand. I reached for it.

There was a new photo in my gallery. One I hadn't taken.

It was me, asleep in my bed, taken from the corner of my room.

I deleted every picture I had with the figure in it. Told the others to do the same. We all agreed... no more group photos. No more risk of seeing it again.

For a while, things seemed normal. We still got together, still hung out, just... without documenting it. I started to relax a little, thinking maybe it was over.

Then last week, my phone buzzed with a notification. A new photo had appeared in my gallery... one from weeks ago, me and Claire at Murphy's. But now, the figure wasn't in the background anymore.

It was standing right behind us.

I turned off my phone. Shoved it in my desk drawer. Told myself I wasn't going to look at it again.

But here's the thing about knowing something like this exists: you can't unknow it. You can't go back to thinking the world works the way you always thought it did.

I still meet up with the others. We're still friends. But something's different now. We're careful about what we capture, what we record. No one takes pictures anymore. No one wants to risk seeing what might be lurking in the background.

Sometimes I catch Claire looking over her shoulder, like she's checking for something. John refuses to have his photo taken by anyone, even family. Ryan's skepticism is gone, replaced by this quiet wariness that never really leaves his eyes.

And me? I've learned to live without photos. Learned to keep memories in my head instead of my phone.

Chapter Twenty-One

The Unlocked Door

"Doors are supposed to keep things out." ~ Alex, Illinois

I've always been careful about locking up at night. Maybe too careful, according to my friends. They used to tease me about my nightly security checks, calling me paranoid. But after what happened in my old apartment, I don't think being paranoid is such a bad thing.

I lived alone in this small one-bedroom on the third floor of my apartment complex. Nothing fancy, but it was clean and quiet, and the neighborhood was decent. I had my routine. Every night before bed, I'd check all the windows, making sure they were locked and the latches were secure. Then I'd check the front door, deadbolt, handle lock. Always in that order. Always twice, just to be sure.

My friends thought I was excessive, but it helped me sleep. I mean, everyone has their quirks, right? Some people need white noise or a nightlight. I needed to know everything was locked up tight.

The morning it started, I was running late for work. I was halfway to the kitchen when the cold hit me. Like someone had left a window open all night.

Then I saw it. My front door was standing wide open.

Not just unlocked... completely open, letting in the outside air. I stood there frozen, my brain trying to process what I was seeing. This wasn't possible. I knew I'd locked up the night before. I always locked up.

I checked everything immediately. The door frame, the locks, looking for any sign of forced entry. Nothing. No damage, no scratches around the locks, nothing out of place in the apartment. My laptop was still on the coffee table. My wallet was still on the counter. Nothing was missing.

I told myself I must have been more tired than I thought the night before. Maybe I'd gone through the motions but hadn't actually turned the locks. It didn't feel right. I could clearly remember checking them twice, like always, but what other explanation could there be?

That night, I was extra thorough. Checked every window twice, then three times. When I got to the front door, I tested each lock multiple times, watching the deadbolt slide into place, listening for that solid click.

The next morning, my heart nearly stopped.

I stood in my hallway, pulse racing, as I tried to make sense of what I was seeing. I knew... I absolutely knew I had locked that door. I checked the locks again. Everything worked perfectly. The deadbolt slid smoothly, the handle lock clicked into place. No signs of tampering.

I called in sick to work and spent the morning watching lock-picking videos online, learning what signs to look for if someone was breaking in. But there was nothing. No scratch marks, no wear patterns, nothing to suggest anyone was forcing their way in.

That evening, I wedged a chair under the doorknob before going to bed. An old trick, but it made me feel better. I even considered sleeping on the couch to keep an eye on things, but I told myself I was being ridiculous. The chair would stop anything from opening that door.

I was wrong.

Something woke me up in the dead of night. Then I heard it. A soft creaking sound from the living room.

I lay perfectly still, listening. For a moment, there was only silence.

Then I heard the chair scrape across the floor.

My whole body tensed up. I reached for my phone, turned on the flashlight, and pointed it toward my bedroom doorway... wishing I had a baseball bat.

Light spilled into the living room, illuminating the front door. The chair had moved several feet away. The door was cracked open, letting in the hallway light.

I bolted out of bed and slammed it shut, hands shaking as I turned all the locks. I spent the rest of the night sitting up, watching that door.

The next day, I bought a security camera. One of those wireless ones that sends alerts to your phone. I set it up facing the door, made sure it had a clear view of the locks. Part of me hoped having it there would stop whatever was happening. Like maybe knowing it was being watched would make it stop.

I barely slept that night, checking my phone every few minutes for alerts. When morning came, I pulled up the footage with shaking hands.

At exactly 2:17 AM, the locks began to move. First the handle, then the deadbolt, turning slowly on their own. No one touched them. No tools, no picks, nothing. They just... turned. Then the door swung open, like someone invisible was walking through.

I watched that footage maybe a hundred times, looking for any explanation. A draft, a problem with the hinges, anything. But there was nothing. Just locks turning themselves and a door opening into an empty hallway.

That night, I decided to stay up and watch. I sat on my couch, all the lights on, staring at that door. As the hours crept by, I felt the exhaustion pulling at me, but I forced myself to stay awake.

Suddenly, I heard the first click.

The handle lock turned, metal scraping against metal. Then the deadbolt began to move, rotating slowly toward the unlocked position. I sat there, paralyzed, watching it happen right in front of me.

The door swung open. The hallway beyond was empty.

I spent that night in a hotel. Called my landlord the next morning and begged to be moved to a different unit. He must have heard the fear in my voice because he didn't even ask questions, just had me sign the paperwork for a unit on the other side of the complex.

I thought moving would fix it. I really did. The new apartment felt different... brighter, somehow. For a week, everything was normal.

Then I woke up again from a dead sleep... my bedroom door was open.

I moved out the next day. Found a place across town, a different complex entirely. Spent way too much breaking my lease, but I didn't care. I had to get out.

After several months of nothing has happening... no doors opening on their own, no locks turning in the night, I could finally relax.

But I still check my locks. Three times now, not just twice. I have cameras on every door in my apartment. And sometimes when I wake up at night, I lay there and listen, wondering if this will be the night I hear that click again.

Doors are supposed to keep things out. But what do you do when something figures out how to get through them anyway? What do you do when locks and bolts mean nothing?

Chapter Twenty-Two
The Silent Radio

"I don't know what to belive... but I listen." ~ Lauren, Alabama

You know those stories about guardian angels? I never believed in them. Too many years working in tech support, I guess... there's usually a logical explanation for everything. But what happened to me... I still can't explain it.

I was driving back from visiting my friend Kate in Millbrook, this tiny town about three hours from the city. It was late, probably close to midnight, and the highway was almost empty.

I remember checking my GPS... still two hours to go. I reached over to turn on the radio, already thinking about what playlist I wanted.

Nothing happened. The display stayed dark.

I frowned, tapping the screen. I'd just used it on the drive out, it had been working fine. I tried the power button again, then the volume knob. Still nothing. Just this blank, dead screen staring back at me.

"Come on," I muttered, hitting the dashboard lightly with my palm. Sometimes that works with temperamental electronics. But the radio stayed silent.

I sighed and settled back in my seat. Just my luck. Two more hours of driving with nothing but engine noise for company.

Then a sound. Just a soft crackle of static through the speakers. I looked at the display... still completely dark. The static faded in and out, like someone slowly turning a dial between stations.

I tried the volume knob again, but it wasn't doing anything. The static continued for maybe another minute, then faded out.

I started humming to myself, some random song I'd had stuck in my head earlier. Anything to break up that weird silence.

The whisper was so faint I almost missed it. Just a breath of sound through the speakers, forming what sounded like my name: "Lauren."

My hands tightened on the steering wheel. The rational part of my brain immediately started making excuses.... interference, crossed signals from another radio, my own imagination. This was something else.

The whispering continued, getting slightly louder. It wasn't coming from any particular direction... it was just there, filling the car.

I jabbed at the power button repeatedly, trying to shut it off. The whispering stopped, but somehow that was worse.

My foot pressed harder on the accelerator. The faster I got home, the better. Trees blurred past my windows, the yellow line on the road seeming to stretch forever. I'd never felt so alone.

Then I heard breathing. Soft, rhythmic breaths coming through the speakers. It sounded so close... like someone was sitting in the passenger seat next to me. I didn't dare look. I didn't want to know what I might see.

I reached for my phone, thinking I'd call Kate, just to hear another human voice. But when I grabbed it from the cup holder, the screen was black. Dead battery. Of course.

The static came back suddenly, louder this time, filling the car with white noise. I was so scared. What the hell was happening?! Then, through the static, that whisper again:

"Slow down."

That's when my headlights caught a deer standing frozen in the middle of the road.

I slammed on the brakes. Time seemed to slow down as I watched the distance between my car and the deer shrink. Please stop, please stop, please—

The car came to a halt just a feet from where the deer stood. It turned and bounded into the darkness, disappearing into the trees.

The radio display flickered to life. The station I'd been listening to earlier started playing, as if nothing had happened.

I pulled over, my whole body shaking. Turned the radio off and on again. It worked perfectly. No static, no whispers. Just normal radio functions.

I sat there, trying to process what had just happened. That voice... it had warned me. Saved me, maybe. If I hadn't slowed down when I did...

"Thank you," I whispered into my car. I felt stupid saying it, but also like I had to. Like whatever had been there needed to know I was grateful.

The rest of the drive home was uneventful. The radio worked fine, playing music like any other night. But I kept glancing at my rearview mirror, half-expecting to see someone in the backseat.

That was six months ago. My radio has never malfunctioned since then. Sometimes I almost convince myself it was just a weird combination of circumstances, a temporary glitch, good timing, an overactive imagination.

But I drive that route pretty regularly, visiting Kate every couple of months. I always whisper "thank you".

I guess sometimes, being alone on a dark highway doesn't mean you're really alone.

I still don't know what to call what happened that night. Guardian angel? Friendly ghost? Random supernatural occurrence? But I do know this: I was supposed to hear that voice. It was trying to help me. And maybe understanding why isn't as important as just being grateful it was there.

These days, I keep my phone charged when I drive at night. But I also keep my radio on. Just in case it needs to tell me something again.

Chapter Twenty-Three

Through Her Eyes

"I keep the bedroom door shut at night." ~ Julia, New York

I tried explaining this story to my therapist once, but I could tell she thought I was having some kind of breakdown. Maybe I was. But that doesn't make what happened any less real.

It's been several years since that weekend at Eleanor's house. Sometimes I wake up in the middle of the night, absolutely certain that someone is standing in my doorway, watching me sleep.

I guess I should start at the beginning. My husband Lucas and I had been married about two years when this happened. His mom Eleanor lived alone in this huge Victorian house a few hours outside the city. The place looked charming when it was built, but now just looked... tired.

We'd visit every few months, usually just for a weekend. I'd always felt weird around Eleanor, but I could never really explain why. You know that feeling when someone's watching you eat? That hyper-aware sensation that makes you suddenly forget how to hold a fork like a normal person? It was like that, all the time. Lucas would laugh it off, say I was imagining things. "Mom's just interested in getting to know you better," he'd say. But there was something else there.

That weekend started like any other visit. We arrived Friday evening, just as the sun was setting. Eleanor met us at the door. She hugged Lucas tight, then turned to me with this half smile.

"Julia, dear," she said. "I've been thinking about you." Something about the way she said it made me uncomfortable.

The house always smelled the same—like old wood. Lucas carried our bags upstairs while Eleanor led me to the dining room, chatting about dinner plans.

That's when the first really weird thing happened. We were sitting at this massive oak table, and Eleanor was serving this roast she'd made. She passed me the plate and said, completely casual, "I made it exactly how you like it, pink in the middle, with extra rosemary. Just like your mother used to make."

I stopped, fork halfway to my mouth. I'd never told Eleanor about my mom's roast. Never mentioned how she'd always add extra rosemary because it was my favorite. My mom died when I was sixteen... long before I met Lucas. I looked at Eleanor, but she was already talking about something else, like she hadn't just said something impossible.

Later that night, it got worse. We were having coffee in the living room when Eleanor started talking about me not sleeping well because of having nightmares. I hadn't told anyone about that. Not even Lucas.

"I just have a good intuition about these things," she said when she caught me staring. Her smile was almost predatory.

I made an excuse about being tired and went up to bed early. Lucas stayed downstairs with his mom.

I was lying in bed, trying to convince myself I was just being paranoid, when I heard them. Footsteps in the hallway, stopping right outside our door. The floorboards creaked like they were leaning closer. But when I got up to check, the hallway was empty.

I must have fallen asleep eventually, but what happened next... I still don't know if it was a dream. It felt too real, too vivid. I was suddenly aware of being in the room, but not in my body. I was standing in the doorway, looking at myself sleeping in the bed. The perspective was all wrong... taller than I am, looking down at my own face from above.

I couldn't look away. I just stood there, watching myself breathe. The worst part was how natural it felt, like I'd done this before. Like I'd been practicing.

I woke up gasping, my heart pounding so hard.

When I went down to breakfast the next morning, Eleanor was already in the kitchen.

"Did you sleep well?" she asked. "I was watching you. You looked so peaceful."

In that moment, everything clicked. The impossible knowledge. The sensation of being watched.

She had been watching me. Not just watching, but like she had been inside my head. And last night I had somehow seen through her eyes as she stood in our doorway, watching me sleep.

I convinced Lucas we needed to leave. I faked being sick, or maybe I really was sick. Everything's a blur until we were in the car, driving away.

That should have been the end of it. We were hours away, safe in our own home. But I just couldn't shake how uncomfortable Eleanor made me feel.

Lucas doesn't understand why I won't visit his mother anymore. How could I explain that she's still watching me, still finding ways into my head?

I haven't told Lucas about that part. I'm afraid if I say it out loud, it'll make it more real.

CHAPTER TWENTY-FOUR

The Black-Eyed Visitors

"I wasn't the only one who saw them." ~ Anonymous, Colorado

I used to love rainy nights. You know, listening to the rain tap against your windows? Yeah. I used to love that. Now, every time it rains after dark, I triple-check my locks and draw all the curtains. I keep telling myself they won't come back.

This happened about 5 years ago, when I was working from home as a web developer. I've always been a night owl... most of my best coding happens after dark when everything is quiet and I can really focus.

The night it happened, we were having a storm. I was deep into debugging this website project, barely even registering the weather anymore, when I heard a knock at my front door.

At first, I thought I'd imagined it. I mean, who'd be out in this weather, especially after midnight?

I remember thinking it had to be my neighbor Erica. Maybe her basement was flooding again, or she needed help with something. But when I looked through the peephole, it wasn't Erica.

Two kids were standing on my porch. A boy, maybe ten or eleven, and what looked like his teenage sister. They were both completely soaked. They weren't moving at all. Just standing there.

Something about the way they were standing made my skin crawl. But they were just kids, right? And it was pouring rain. What kind of person would I be if I left them out there?

"Hello?" I called through the door. "Are you okay?"

They spoke in perfect unison with zero emotion in their voices. "We need to use your phone."

Their voices... everything about it felt rehearsed, mechanical.

"Where are your parents?" I asked, trying to keep my voice steady. "Are you lost?"

They didn't answer my question. But, they spoke again, "Let us in."

Every horror movie I'd ever seen was screaming in my head, but they were just kids. Just kids who needed help. Right?

"I can call someone for you," I offered. "The police, or..."

"Let us in."

Their voices were different now. Like they were becoming impatient. And then... then they looked up.

I'll never forget what I saw through that peephole. Their eyes were completely black. Not just the iris or pupil... the entire eye. My legs went weak, and I immediately questioned if my eyes were playing tricks on me.

The doorknob started turning. It was locked, so they couldn't get in, but they were trying to open the door.

I ran. I'm not ashamed to admit it. I ran to my kitchen, feeling like I needed to hide, but not exactly sure what to do.

Then everything went quiet.

I stood there, shaking, for what felt like hours but was probably only minutes. Finally, I found enough courage to check the front door again. They were gone. The porch was empty.

The relief lasted about three seconds... until I heard knocking at my back door.

"Let us in."

I heard fingernails scraping gently against the door, a sound that made my teeth ache.

I turned on every light in the house. Told them to go away or I'd call the police. The knocking stopped, but I didn't sleep. How could I?

They came back a few more times. Sometimes at the front door, sometimes at the back. Once, I heard them knocking on my bedroom window.

I didn't last long before I moved. Erica, my neighbor, caught me while I was loading the U-Haul. She asked if I'd seen "those poor kids" standing in the rain. Said she'd called the police about them, but when the cops showed up, there was no one there.

I live in an apartment downtown now. Fourteenth floor. No way anyone could reach my windows. I haven't heard the knocking in months. Haven't seen any children with black eyes standing in the rain.

CHAPTER TWENTY-FIVE

The Neighbor's Light

"Sometimes you feel someone watching." ~ Graham, California

I used to live in an apartment that was a one-bedroom unit in a U-shaped complex, where all the windows faced the central courtyard. From my living room, I had a clear view of the apartment directly across from mine, where Mr. Whitaker lived. He was this gentle old man, probably in his late seventies, who spent his evenings in this leather recliner next to a floor lamp.

Every night around ten-thirty, like clockwork, I'd look up from whatever I was doing and see him there. Sometimes reading a thick hardcover book, sometimes watching TV with his reading glasses perched on the end of his nose. He'd always notice me looking and give this warm, grandfatherly smile and a little wave. I'd nod back, and that was it.

I started noticing things. Like how Mr. Whitaker was always sitting at exactly the same angle. How his wave was identical every single time.

I found myself watching more carefully, trying to catch variations that never came. Every night, same position, same smile, same wave. Like watching a video loop over and over.

Then one day came the knock at my door.

When I opened the door, there was a man about my age standing there, looking tired and slightly uncomfortable.

"Hi," he said, "I'm David Whitaker. My father lived across the way?"

The past tense hit me like a punch to the gut.

"I just wanted to let the neighbors know we'll be clearing out Dad's apartment this week," he continued. "I didn't want you to worry if you see strangers going in and out of his apartment."

I asked. "Clearing out? Is Mr. Whitaker moving to a facility?"

"No, I'm sorry... my father passed away. A little over a week ago."

The world tilted sideways. "That's impossible. I saw him last night. In his chair, reading. He waved to me."

David went very still.

" I appreciate you being kind about my father, but that's not possible. Dad died nine days ago. Heart attack, right there in his apartment. We've had it locked up ever since, until we could get movers arranged."

I wanted to argue, to tell him he was wrong. But I didn't want to argue with the man who was going through the loss of a parent. Plus, he was going to think I wasn't right in the head.

"I'm sorry for your loss," I said. He thanked me and left. My mind was racing, trying to make sense of what I'd just learned. Because I knew what I'd seen every night.

Didn't I?

That night, I sat there, staring at Mr. Whitaker's window. The apartment was pitch black, had been all day. No lamp, no TV glow, no movement. Just emptiness and shadows.

At 8:28 PM, the lamp clicked on. Maybe it was on a timer?

But there, in the recliner, was Mr. Whitaker.

My chest went tight. I couldn't do anything but stare as he slowly turned his head toward my window. His eyes were dark hollows, his mouth slightly open as if trying to speak.

He raised his hand... that familiar gesture I'd seen a hundred times before. But this time it wasn't a wave. He was gesturing for me to come over.

The lamp went out.

I think I might have screamed. I spent the rest of the night huddling in my bedroom, every light on.

I moved out a couple of months later. Couldn't stand being there anymore, couldn't bear to look at that window every night. My new place is on the ground floor of a garden apartment complex. No windows facing other units, no chance of seeing lights in the night.

I keep my blinds closed after dark now.

Chapter Twenty-Six
The Woman in the Stairwell

"I don't take the stairs anymore." ~ Anonymous, California

I've worked security for fifteen years, and in all that time, I've only been truly afraid once. Not the kind of fear that makes you jump at shadows or check behind doors. The kind that makes you question everything you thought you knew about reality.

Most people don't understand what it's like working nights in a big office building. Sure, they've stayed late once or twice, maybe came in on a weekend when things were quiet. But that's not the same as being there at three in the morning.

I used to love the silence, actually. Fifteen years of night shifts, mostly in those tall buildings that fill up downtown. They turn into ghost towns after six PM. There's something peaceful about walking through a silent building at night, checking doors, making sure everything's secure. Well... I used to think it was peaceful. Now? Now I won't even take night shifts anymore. Won't use stairwells either, if I can help it.

Before I tell you what happened that night, you need to understand something about night security work. It's not like in the movies, where guards sit in their office watching cameras all night, waiting for something to happen. Real security work is active. You walk your rounds, check every floor, make sure all the doors are secure. You get to know a building.

I'd been working there about four years. Fourteen floors of mostly investment firms and insurance companies, with a couple of tech startups scattered through the middle floors. Four stairwells, six elevators, and a layout like an L, with the longest wing facing the river.

My shift started at 10 PM, right after the cleaning crew finished up. Standard routine... start at the top floor, work my way down, checking that all exterior doors were secure, no lights left on. Then a second walkthrough around 3 AM, just to make sure nothing had changed. We were supposed to use the stairs unless we were responding to an alarm to make sure no one was hiding or sleeping in there.

I usually stuck to the main stairwell near the elevators. It was the widest, with windows every landing that looked out over the river. Those windows were important, they let in enough light that you didn't feel like you were walking into a tomb. The other stairwells were narrower, darker, with just emergency lighting to guide you. I avoided those when I could.

That night, March 15th, 2023, I'll never forget the date, started like any other. The weather report had been calling for storms all week, but so far it was just this endless drizzle.

I remember checking my watch as I started my second round. A little early, but I had paperwork to finish before my shift ended at six. The top floor was clear, just rows of cubicles and dark conference rooms. Nothing out of place.

I was maybe four floors down when I first saw her.

She was a couple of floors below me, moving down the stairs at this weird pace. Not exactly slow, but not normal either. She was wearing what a dress and she was barefoot. That detail stuck with me, those pale feet against the concrete steps.

At first, I tried to rationalize it. Sometimes people got locked out of their offices while taking a call in the stairwell. It happened often enough that we had a procedure for it. So I asked, "Ma'am? Building's closed. Do you need help?"

She didn't respond. Seemed like she didn't even hear me. Just kept descending.

I picked up my pace, trying to catch up. That's when things got strange. The acoustics in stairwells are weird. Everything echoes. My boots were making this loud clacking sound with every step, bouncing off the walls. But her? Nothing. Not a single noise. No movement, not footsteps, nothing.

And no matter how fast I walked, I couldn't seem to get any closer. Every time I'd reach a landing where I'd just seen her, she'd already be three floors down. It was like... like trying to catch up to your own shadow. The harder I tried, the more impossible it seemed.

By the time I hit the fifth floor, my heart was pounding. Not from exertion... from fear. Because I knew by now, that whatever I was following wasn't normal. The way she moved, the silence, none of it was right.

When I finally reached the ground floor, the stairwell door was just swinging shut. I burst through it, ready to... I don't know what. Confront her? Help her? Run? But the hallway was empty. Completely empty.

I ran to the security office. Had to know if I was losing my mind. We had cameras in the stairwells... old ones, black and white, but they worked. I pulled up the footage from the last ten minutes.

There I was, entering from the top floor. There I was, calling out, speeding up, chasing... nothing. The footage showed me completely alone in that stairwell. But those doors at the bottom of the stairwell opened and closed by themselves.

I sat there for a long time, just staring at that footage. Trying to make sense of it. Trying to convince myself there was some logical explanation. But I knew what I'd seen. That woman, she'd been there. Just not in any way that cameras could capture.

The rest of that shift was hell. I kept feeling like if I turned around fast enough, I'd catch her standing behind me.

I didn't tell anyone. I mean, how could I? "Hey, I saw a ghost in the stairwell"? Security work isn't exactly friendly to that kind of talk. But then things started happening that I couldn't ignore.

The next week, I was doing my rounds when there she was, at the end of the hallway, standing perfectly still. Just... watching. I turned and ran for the elevator..

After that, it was like a dam broke. Other guards started reporting things too. One said he kept hearing footsteps in empty hallways. Another, who covered weekends, reported doors opening and closing on their own. That feeling of being watched... it became a regular topic during shift changes.

Then came the night that broke me. I was almost to twelve when I heard it... the soft rustle above me. I looked up through the center of the stairwell, and there she was, looking down at me from the next landing. Just... standing there.

I ran. Didn't even try to play it cool. Just turned and sprinted down those stairs like the devil himself was chasing me. I quit my job the next day.

Found a new job at a smaller building, single story, no stairwells, and most importantly... day shift. I can't handle being alone in buildings after dark.

Chapter Twenty-Seven

The Baby Monitor

"Nothing gets that close to my child again." ~ Evelyn, Florida

My son is seven now. Old enough that I don't need to watch him constantly, don't need to check on him multiple times a night. But I still do. I can't help it. Even though we moved away from the house that this story happened in, and nothing strange has happened since, I still wake up worried that something is in his room.

Five years ago, I was a newly single mom with a two-year-old son, Eli. His father wasn't in the picture, and I was doing my best to juggle full-time remote work with being a mom. It wasn't easy, but we had our routine. Our little two-bedroom rental wasn't fancy, but it was cozy. Enough space for the two of us.

The house was old but not scary. Nothing that made me nervous. I'd even checked the neighborhood crime stats before moving in... they were some of the lowest in the city.

Eli was a good sleeper, thank God. But I was still paranoid about something happening to him while I was working in my home office. So, I bought this fancy baby monitor, one of those with a camera and night vision, so I could check on him without having to open his door and risk waking him up.

The first couple weeks were great. I could see him sleeping peacefully in his crib, occasionally rolling over or mumbling in his sleep. Sometimes he'd wake up and play quietly with his stuffed giraffe before falling asleep again. Normal toddler stuff. The monitor actually helped me relax a little, knowing I could check on him anytime.

Looking back now, I realize the strange things started so gradually I almost didn't notice. The monitor would sometimes get static-y, even though the WiFi signal was strong. Eli started waking up at around 1:00 AM several nights in a row... not crying, just... awake. Staring at something I couldn't see.

I remember the first time I noticed something truly odd. I was working late, and Eli had been asleep for hours. The monitor caught my eye because he was doing this weird little wave, not his usual excited toddler wave, but this movement, like he was copying someone. He'd pause, then wave again, like he was taking turns. There was nobody else in the room, but he was completely focused on the empty corner by his dresser.

A few nights later, I heard him giggling through the monitor around midnight. When I checked the screen, he was sitting up, pointing at different toys and naming them: "Ball... car... bear..." But the weird part was, he'd pause after each one like he was waiting for a response. Then he'd clap his hands, as if someone had praised him.

These little incidents kept happening. I'd catch him having what seemed like conversations, but only his side was audible. He'd ask questions like "What color?" or "Where go?" followed by intense listening and then reactions to something I couldn't hear. Sometimes he'd nod seriously, like he was receiving instructions. Other times he'd laugh and say "Again, again!" to the empty room.

One night, I was watching him play this apparent game of peek-a-boo with nothing. He'd cover his eyes, then uncover them with a delighted "There!"

I started keeping a log of these incidents, trying to convince myself there were logical explanations. Maybe he was sleep-talking.

One night I was half-listening to the monitor while answering emails when I heard him say, clear as day: "Pretty lady." I looked up to see him reaching toward that same corner again.

"What lady?" I asked through the monitor's talk-back feature.

"Lady sing me songs," he said, still looking at the corner.

My blood ran cold. Before I could respond, he added: "She says shhhhh now. Night-night time."

And just like that, he laid down and went to sleep.

After that night, the incidents became more frequent. I'd hear him having longer conversations with his unseen friend. He'd ask her to sing specific songs... lullabies I'd never taught him.

I heard him say: "No, don't cry. I here."

But then came the whispers. That soft, gentle "Shhh..." that I'd hear through the monitor whenever Eli was restless. It wasn't me. I was nowhere near his room. It wasn't him. The sound was distinctly feminine, almost musical. But it would calmed him instantly, like a mother's touch.

The next night was worse. I'd stayed up late to watch the monitor, determined to catch whatever was happening. Around 2 AM, I noticed the crib moving. Not violently... just a gentle rocking motion, like someone was trying to soothe him. But Eli was completely still, sound asleep.

Then I saw it. A shadow, darker than the other darkness in the room, moving near the crib. It wasn't sharp or defined. But it was there. It was real.

I ran to his room, my heart pounding so hard I thought it might explode. Threw open the door, flipped on the lights... nothing. The room was perfectly still. Eli hadn't even stirred.

I checked the monitor footage again. And there it was... just before I entered, the nursery door had opened on its own. Slowly, silently, like someone invisible had turned the handle and pushed it open.

I grabbed Eli and brought him to my room that night. And every night after. I couldn't leave him alone in there, not after what I'd seen. What if... what if whatever it was decided to do more than just watch him?

People told me I was being paranoid. That old houses make weird noises, that baby monitors can pick up interference. But they hadn't seen what I saw. Hadn't heard that whispered "Shhh" in the darkness.

We moved a month later. I couldn't take it anymore, the constant checking, the fear every time night fell, that feeling of being watched.

He's seven now, and thankfully doesn't seem to remember anything about the lady.

I've learned to live with never knowing if what watched over my son was something dangerous or just... something lost. Something that found a small measure of peace in caring for another mother's child.

But I never used baby monitors again. Haven't since that night.

Sometimes I think about researching the history of that old house, trying to find out if any mother ever lost a child there. But I never do. Because I'm afraid of what I might find.

Because then I'd have to face the fact that for months, I left my baby alone with something that wasn't human. And even though nothing bad ever happened, I'll never forgive myself for not recognizing the signs sooner.

Chapter Twenty-Eight

The Customer Who Never Left

"I work at an office now." ~ Anonymous, Oklahoma

I worked the night shift at Eddie's Diner for almost four years. The kind of place where truckers stop at 3 AM for eggs and hash browns.

It wasn't a bad job, really. The tips weren't great, but the regulars were decent, and I liked the quiet.

That's probably why it took me so long to notice something was wrong about him. About the man in booth seven.

I don't know exactly when it started. That's the thing that bothers me most now. I can't pinpoint the first time I saw him. He was just... there one night.

Sitting in that corner booth by the window, coffee cup in front of him, staring out at the empty parking lot.

He wasn't memorable at first. Middle-aged, I guess, wearing one of those plain button-down shirts that office workers wear. The kind of customer you see a hundred times a week. He'd give this slight nod when I'd refill his coffee, but never spoke. Never ordered food. Just sat there with his coffee, watching the world outside that window.

I figured he was another lonely soul seeking company without conversation. We got a lot of those on night shift. People who just needed to be somewhere that wasn't home, you know? So I'd check his cup, give him refills when needed, let him be.

But after a while... I started noticing how I never actually saw him walk in. He'd just be there when I turned around, sitting quietly in booth seven. I never saw him leave either. I'd get busy with other customers or head to the kitchen, and when I looked again, he'd be gone. His coffee cup would be there, still full, but ice cold.

I tried to remember if I'd ever heard the door chime when he arrived or left. If I'd ever handed him a menu or taken his order that first time. But it was like trying to remember a dream.

Then I started noticing the way the vinyl seat never creaked when he shifted position. How I never heard the clink of his cup against the saucer.

One night, I was in the middle of my usual rounds when I realized something else: I'd never actually seen him drink the coffee. I mean, I'd seen him holding the cup countless times, lifting it maybe, but I'd never seen it touch his lips. Never seen the level of coffee in the cup go down.

I told myself I was being ridiculous. That I was just tired, that the late hours were making me imagine things.

One night it was really slow. Really slow, just me and Carol working. Around 2 AM, I grabbed the coffee pot for my rounds. He was there in booth seven, same as always. I walked over, pot ready to pour, when Carol called out from behind the counter.

"Who are you talking to?"

I turned to look at her, confused. "What do you mean? The customer in booth seven."

Carol frowned. "Honey, there's nobody there. That booth's been empty all night."

I looked back at the booth, and... she was right. It was empty. The coffee cup was there, full to the brim and ice cold, but the man was gone. My hands started shaking so bad I had to set the coffee pot down.

"But he was just here, I was about to..." I couldn't finish the sentence. Because now that I thought about it, really thought about it, I couldn't remember ever giving him a bill or taking his payment.

Carol must have seen something in my face because she came over and touched my arm. "You okay? You're white as a sheet."

I tried to explain about the quiet man who'd been coming in for... how long had it been? Weeks? Months? But as I talked, I realized how crazy it sounded. A customer who never ate, never really drank his coffee, never spoke, who no one else had ever seen.

After that night, I'd still see him sometimes, but only from the corner of my eye. The moment I tried to look directly at booth seven, he'd be gone.

But I'd hear things... the soft squeak of vinyl as if someone was shifting in the seat, the quiet tap of a coffee cup being set down.

One night, near the end of my shift, I got this overwhelming urge to sit in booth seven. Just to see what he'd been staring at all those nights.

That's when I noticed the small brass plaque on the wall next to the booth. I'd seen it a hundred times but never really looked at it before. It was one of those memorial things some diners put up for long-time customers who've passed.

"In Memory of Richard White

1947-2012

A faithful friend who always brightened our mornings"

There was a small photo beneath the text.

It was him. The quiet man from booth seven. The photo showed him younger, smiling, but it was definitely him. Same button-down shirt, same gentle eyes.

I quit the next day. I couldn't... I just couldn't face booth seven anymore. Couldn't handle the thought that I'd been serving coffee to someone who'd died years before I even started working there.

That was seven years ago. I work in an office now.

www.ingramcontent.com/pod-product-compliance
Lightning Source LLC
Chambersburg PA
CBHW020542030426
42337CB00013B/950